Table of Content

Table of Content 1

Chapter 1: Introduction to Machine Learning 5

1.1 Understanding the Core Concepts and Definitions 9

1.2 Historical Evolution and Milestones 12

1.3 Key Components: Algorithms, Models, and Data 15

1.4 The Impact of Machine Learning on Various Industries 18

Chapter 2: Types of Machine Learning 21

2.1 Supervised Learning: Principles and Applications 24

2.2 Unsupervised Learning: Clustering and Association 27

2.3 Reinforcement Learning: Fundamentals and Realworld Scenarios 30

2.4 Hybrid Learning Approaches and Choosing the Right Model ... 34

Chapter 3: Data Exploration and Preprocessing 38

3.1 The Role of Data in Machine Learning 41

3.2 Exploratory Data Analysis (EDA) Techniques 44

3.3 Data Cleaning and Handling Missing Values 47

3.4 Feature Engineering: Optimizing Data for Models 50

Chapter 4: Model Development and Training 55

4.1 Overview of Model Building 58

4.2 Algorithm Selection and Model Architecture 61

4.3 Data Splitting for Training and Validation 65

4.4 HandsOn: Building and Training Your First Model 68

Chapter 5: Model Evaluation and Metrics 71

5.1 The Importance of Robust Model Evaluation 74

5.2 Common Evaluation Metrics: Accuracy, Precision, Recall 77

5.3 Receiver Operating Characteristic (ROC) Curve 81

5.4 Interpreting Evaluation Results and Model Selection 84

Chapter 6: Feature Selection and Importance............................ 88

6.1 Understanding Feature Significance 92

6.2 Techniques for Feature Selection... 95

6.3 Handling Categorical and Numerical Features 98

6.4 Best Practices in Feature Engineering 102

Chapter 7: Neural Networks and Deep Learning....................... 105

7.1 Introduction to Neural Networks.. 108

7.2 Core Components: Layers, Neurons, and Weights 110

7.3 Activation Functions and Backpropagation 113

7.4 Basic Architectures: Feedforward and Recurrent Networks . 116

Chapter 8: Deep Learning Applications.................................... 120

8.1 Distinguishing Deep Learning from Traditional ML 124

8.2 Convolutional Neural Networks (CNNs) for Image Tasks...... 127

8.3 Natural Language Processing (NLP) with Recurrent Networks 131

8.4 Realworld Applications and Success Stories 135

Chapter 9: Model Deployment Strategies 138

9.1 Transitioning from Development to Deployment.................. 142

9.2 Common Deployment Platforms and Best Practices 146

9.3 Scaling Models for Production 151

9.4 Continuous Monitoring and Maintenance Strategies............ 154

Chapter 10: Ethical Considerations in Machine Learning........... 158

10.1 Navigating Ethical Challenges in ML.................................. 161

10.2 Addressing Bias and Fairness in Algorithms 165

10.3 Ensuring Transparency and Accountability 169

10.4 Legal and Ethical Implications in Model Deployment 172

Chapter 11: Resources for Continuous Learning 175

11.1 Recommended Books, Courses, and Online Platforms 178

11.2 Engaging with the Machine Learning Community 181

11.3 Participating in Conferences and Workshops 184

11.4 Cultivating a Lifelong Learning Mindset 187

Chapter 12: Future Trends in Machine Learning 190

12.1 Exploring Emerging Technologies in ML 193

12.2 The Role of Explainable AI and Model Interpretability 196

12.3 Integration of AI in Industry 4.0 199

12.4 Preparing for the Future: Key Considerations 203

Chapter 13: Realworld Applications and Case Studies 206

13.1 Applications Across Industries: Healthcare, Finance, and more 209

13.2 Success Stories and Case Studies 212

13.3 Challenges Faced in Realworld Deployments 215

13.4 Inspiring Examples of Machine Learning Impact 218

Chapter 14: Challenges and Limitations in ML 221

14.1 Recognizing Common Challenges in ML 224

14.2 Strategies for Overcoming Model Limitations 228

14.3 Data Quality and Quantity Constraints 231

14.4 Continuous Improvement for Sustainable ML 234

Chapter 15: Building a Machine Learning Portfolio 237

15.1 Importance of a Machine Learning Portfolio 240

15.2 Showcasing Projects and Practical Applications 243

15.3 Documenting Model Development Process 246

15.4 Enhancing Employability with a Strong ML Portfolio 250

Chapter 1: Introduction to Machine Learning

Amidst the details of this chapter, we will introduce the basic concepts and foundations of this thriving field. Whether you are a student, a professional looking to switch careers, or simply someone interested in understanding the fundamentals of machine learning, this chapter will lay a solid groundwork for your journey ahead.

1. 1 What is Machine Learning.
Machine learning is a subset of artificial intelligence that focuses on empowering computer systems to learn and improve from experience without being explicitly programmed. Rather than relying on predetermined rules or specific instructions, machine learning algorithms enable systems to analyze data, identify patterns, and generate insights or predictions.

1. 2 The Importance of Machine Learning
Machine learning has revolutionized various industries, such as healthcare, finance, manufacturing, and marketing, by providing robust tools for data analysis and decision-making. It has transformed how companies optimize their operations, make accurate forecasts, personalize user experiences, detect fraud, and improve overall efficiency.

1. 3 Types of Machine Learning
There are several types of machine learning algorithms, each catering to different computational problems and contexts. Let's explore the three fundamental categories:

1. 3. 1 Supervised Learning
Supervised learning involves training a model using labeled data,

in which input variables are paired with the correct output variables. The algorithm learns from these examples and can predict the output for new, unseen data. Typical supervised learning tasks include classification (predicting discrete labels) and regression (predicting continuous values).

1. 3. 2 Unsupervised Learning

Unsupervised learning addresses scenarios where the data is unlabeled, meaning there are no predetermined output variables. Algorithms attempt to identify patterns and structures in the data by clustering similar data points together or by reducing the dimensionality of the data. Unsupervised learning is primarily used for exploratory analysis and data visualization purposes.

1. 3. 3 Reinforcement Learning

Reinforcement learning involves training an agent to interact with its environment and learn from feedback in the form of rewards or penalties. The agent explores different actions over time, aiming to maximize its cumulative reward. Reinforcement learning algorithms are crucial in complex tasks, such as game playing, robotics, and optimizing business strategies.

1. 4 Key Steps in Machine Learning

Understanding the complete life cycle of a machine learning project is essential for achieving successful outcomes. Here are some crucial steps commonly followed:

1. 4. 1 Problem Definition and Data Collection

Clearly define the problem you want to solve and gather relevant data to train your model. Determine the specific challenges and objectives of your project, ensuring proper assortment and quality of data for effective learning.

1. 4. 2 Data Preprocessing

Raw data often contains irrelevant or noisy information that can adversely affect model performance. Data preprocessing involves cleaning, transforming, and normalizing data to ensure its quality and integrity. This step is crucial to eliminate biases and inconsistent patterns, improving the robustness of subsequent analyses.

1.4.3 Feature Engineering and Selection
Feature engineering involves selecting or creating the most informative input data, known as features, that will contribute to training your model effectively. This step requires domain expertise and creativity to extract the most relevant information, reducing noise, and facilitating accurate predictions.

1.4.4 Model Selection and Training
Choosing an appropriate machine learning model requires a thorough understanding of the problem and the characteristics of different algorithms. This step involves splitting the labeled data into training and validation sets to train, fine-tune, and evaluate the model's performance.

1.4.5 Model Evaluation and Validation
Once the model is trained, it needs to be evaluated for its effectiveness using appropriate metrics and evaluation techniques. This step ensures that the model generalizes well to new, unseen data, rather than purely memorizing the training examples.

1.4.6 Model Deployment and Monitoring
The final step involves deploying the trained model into a production environment, often integrated within a larger software system. Continuous monitoring and assessment ensure that the model performs as expected, and regular updates are made to enhance its performance over time.

1.5 Ethical Considerations in Machine Learning
As machine learning becomes increasingly ingrained in our daily lives, it raises ethical concerns that need to be addressed. Issues like privacy, bias, and fairness should be taken into account to build responsible and unbiased machine learning systems. It is crucial to ensure transparency, accountability, and fairness throughout the entire machine learning pipeline.

In Chapter 1, we have covered the fundamental concepts of machine learning, its importance, types of algorithms, and key steps involved in a typical machine learning project. In the following chapters, we will dive deeper into each category, exploring popular algorithms, practical implementation techniques, and advanced concepts to equip you with a comprehensive understanding of machine learning. So, buckle up and get ready to embark on an exciting journey of acquiring machine learning expertise.

1.1 Understanding the Core Concepts and Definitions

Machine learning, a fascinating and rapidly evolving field, has revolutionized various industries with its ability to automate processes, detect patterns, and make predictions based on data. To embark on your journey into machine learning, it is crucial to grasp the core concepts and definitions that underpin this domain.

Machine learning can be defined as the ability of a computer system to improve its performance on a particular task by pattern recognition and continuous learning from data, without being explicitly programmed for that task. In other words, instead of having a programmer provide the specific instructions for every possible scenario, machine learning algorithms develop their own logic by analyzing the available data.

One of the fundamental concepts in machine learning is the notion of a model, which represents the knowledge captured from the data. The model is refined iteratively as it ingests more data, allowing it to make increasingly accurate predictions. The mechanism of constructing a model from input data is known as the learning algorithm.

When discussing machine learning, it is important to understand the distinction between labeled and unlabeled data. Labeled data is a dataset where each example has a corresponding class or output label associated with it. By contrast, unlabeled data lacks these labels but is still valuable for various tasks such as clustering, where the goal is to group similar data points together without explicit class assignments.

Supervised learning and unsupervised learning are the two

overarching paradigms in machine learning. Supervised learning involves training a model on labeled data, allowing it to learn the relationship between the input features and their corresponding labels. This knowledge enables the model to make predictions on new, unseen data.

On the other hand, unsupervised learning algorithms aim to discover hidden patterns or structures in the data without using any predefined labels. The models learn from the inherent structure of the dataset and identify similarities or regularities among the data instances. Unsupervised learning algorithms are commonly used for tasks like clustering, anomaly detection, and dimensionality reduction.

To evaluate the performance of machine learning models and compare them objectively, we need metrics such as accuracy, precision, recall, and F1 score. These metrics provide insights into how well the model generalizes to new, unseen data and helps in choosing the most suitable algorithm for a given problem.

Overfitting and underfitting are crucial concepts to understand. Overfitting occurs when a machine learning model performs exceptionally well on the training data but fails to generalize to unseen data. This can happen when the model becomes overly complex and starts memorizing the training examples instead of learning the underlying patterns. Underfitting, conversely, happens when the model is too simplistic to capture the complexities present in the data, resulting in poor performance both on the training and test data.

Feature engineering is another critical aspect of machine learning. It involves selecting or creating appropriate features from the available raw data to improve the predictive performance of the models. Effective feature engineering can significantly enhance the model's ability to extract useful information and patterns from the data.

Regularization is a technique used to prevent overfitting in machine learning models. It imposes a penalty on complex models, discouraging them from learning unnecessary or noisy features. Using regularization techniques, such as L1 or L2 regularization, can lead to more balanced models with improved generalization on unseen data.

The understanding of these core concepts and definitions will provide you with a solid foundation for your machine learning journey. Through continued exploration and hands-on practice, you will unravel the intricacies of advanced machine learning techniques, enabling you to solve complex problems and make data-driven decisions with confidence.

1.2 Historical Evolution and Milestones

Historical Evolution and Milestones in Machine Learning
Machine learning, an interdisciplinary field at the intersection of computer science and statistics, has gained significant momentum in recent decades. It has allowed us to enable intelligent systems capable of autonomously learning, adapting, and improving without explicit programming. The rich historical evolution and milestones of machine learning showcase the journey, breakthroughs, and paradigm shifts that have shaped this field into what it is today.

1. Early Origins:
Machine learning finds its roots in artificial intelligence (AI). The concept of teaching machines to learn from data and make intelligent decisions emerged in the mid-20th century. Early developments witnessed the emergence of logical AI systems such as expert systems, rule-based systems, and decision trees. The major challenge was to make these systems self-adaptive and capable of learning from data, giving birth to the thinking around machine learning.

2. Foundational Concepts:
The evolution of machine learning became more pronounced in the second half of the 20th century. Key conceptual frameworks, algorithms, and approaches laid the foundation for further progress. The perceptron, proposed by Frank Rosenblatt in 1957, sparked interest in neural networks and pattern recognition. This seminal work set the stage for deep learning much later.

3. Statistical Learning Theory:
Machine learning became more theoretically grounded in the 1960s and 1970s. Arthur Samuel's path-breaking work in the 1960s on machine learning, using a game of checkers to train models, emphasized the importance of data-driven training.

4. Rise of Decision Trees and Rule-Based Systems:
The early 1980s saw the development of decision tree algorithms such as ID3 by Ross Quinlan and the subsequent C4. 5 algorithm. Decision trees allowed for hierarchical decision-making based on input features, enabling clearer explanations and interpretability. Alongside decision trees, the expert systems built around rule-based systems (e. g. , MYCIN, DENDRAL) paved the way for knowledge-driven machine learning.

5. Reinforcement Learning:
The idea of reinforcement learning, where an agent learns through environmental feedback, took off in the late 1980s and early 1990s. This approach introduced the concept of reward-based learning, enabling systems to learn optimal actions in dynamic environments. Reinforcement learning is widely applied in various fields, including gaming, robotics, and optimization problems with numerous possible actions.

6. Support Vector Machines and Kernel Methods:
In the mid-1990s, support vector machines (SVM) emerged as a powerful algorithm within the sphere of supervised learning. SVMs use the concept of hyperplanes to classify data efficiently, based on separating different classes. Simultaneously, kernel methods introduced by Alexander Mercer expanded the applicability of SVMs by mapping data into higher-dimensional spaces, enabling nonlinear classification.

7. Deep Learning and Neural Networks:
The early 2000s witnessed a resurgence of interest in neural networks with the advent of deep learning. The development of more effective training algorithms (e. g. , backpropagation, stochastic gradient descent) and the increase in computational power enabled training of deep neural networks with multiple hidden layers. Techniques like convolutional neural networks (CNN) revolutionized image recognition, recurrent neural networks (RNN) improved natural language processing, and generative adversarial networks (GAN) set new benchmarks in generating realistic content.

8. Unsupervised Learning and Clustering:
The advancements in unsupervised learning brought about robust techniques for discovering patterns and hidden structures within data. Clustering algorithms like k-means, hierarchical clustering, and density-based spatial clustering introduced mechanisms to group data points into meaningful clusters, aiding exploratory data analysis, customer segmentation, and anomaly detection.

9. Transfer Learning and Few-shot Learning:
In recent years, transfer learning has gained prominence, leveraging pre-trained models to solve new tasks with limited training data. By leveraging the learned representations from highly specialized models trained on large datasets, transfer learning expedites learning on smaller datasets and promotes efficient knowledge transfer across domains. Additionally, few-shot learning deals with training models to learn from a few examples rapidly, reflecting the limited availability of labeled data in many real-world scenarios.

Conclusion:
The historical evolution and numerous milestones achieved in machine learning have transformed the field from a theoretical concept into a reality with widespread practical implementations. Understanding these past developments equips beginners with valuable insights into the fundamental concepts, enabling them to explore the vast landscape of machine learning with a historical context.

1.3 Key Components: Algorithms, Models, and Data

Machine learning, at its core, deals with the interplay of three crucial components: algorithms, models, and data. Understanding these key components is essential for anyone starting their journey into the world of machine learning. Amidst this section, we will delve deep into each of these components and explore their role in building successful machine learning systems.

Algorithms:

Algorithms form the heart of machine learning, as they encode the underlying logic and instructions that enable machines to learn. In the context of machine learning, an algorithm is a set of mathematical and statistical rules that govern the behavior of machine learning models. These rules guide the learning process by identifying patterns, relationships, and hidden structures in the data.

There exists a wide range of machine learning algorithms, each designed to handle specific types of problems. Some fundamental algorithms include linear regression, decision trees, support vector machines, k-nearest neighbors, and neural networks. Each algorithm possesses its own set of strengths and weaknesses, making it suitable for particular tasks.

When choosing an algorithm, one should consider factors like the nature of the problem, the characteristics of the data, and the desired outcome. It is important to understand that algorithms serve as a foundation upon which models are built, and the performance of these models depends heavily on the appropriateness of the chosen algorithm.

Models:

Machine learning models are representations of real-world systems that enable us to reason and make predictions about unseen data. Models are constructed by training algorithms on a set of input data, enabling them to learn the underlying patterns and relationships present within. Once trained, the model can be used to infer or generalize upon unseen data, leading to predictions, classifications, or clustering.

Models can take various forms, depending on the specific algorithm used. For instance, linear regression produces a linear model, while decision trees create a hierarchical structure of decision nodes. More complex algorithms like neural networks generate intricate interconnected models.

The aim of a machine learning model is to extract generalizable knowledge from data and make accurate predictions on unseen samples. Model performance can be measured using evaluation metrics such as accuracy, precision, and recall. Assessing model performance is paramount, as it aids in understanding whether the model is reliably capturing the underlying patterns in the data.

Data:

Data is the lifeblood of any machine learning system. It acts as the fuel that drives the learning process and informs the decision-making of algorithms. In machine learning, data can be divided into two primary categories: training data and testing data.

Training data is a labeled dataset used to train machine learning models. It contains a set of input samples, typically paired with corresponding output or target values. The algorithm uses this data to learn patterns and build a model capable of generalization. It is essential to have a diverse and representative training dataset, as it ensures the model learns a broad understanding of the problem domain.

Testing data, on the other hand, is an unlabeled dataset used to evaluate the performance of trained models. This data serves as a proxy for real-world scenarios where the model will encounter unseen examples. Evaluating a model's accuracy on this data is crucial to gauge its predictive power and ensure it can make reliable forecasts.

High-quality data is central to the success of any machine learning project. Data must be clean, well-structured, and meaningful to ensure the model can derive useful insights. Perform data preprocessing tasks such as removing outliers, handling missing values, and normalizing the data before feeding it into the learning algorithm.

Remember that data is a constant evolving entity and acquiring new data can improve the performance of machine learning models. Continuous evaluation, refinement, and updating of the data are necessary to ensure models remain robust and effective over time.

In conclusion, machine learning hinges on its three core components: algorithms, models, and data. These components work in unison to root out patterns within data and enable desired outcomes. By effectively selecting appropriate algorithms, constructing accurate models, and working with high-quality data, one can build powerful machine learning systems capable of insightful predictions and reliable decision-making.

1.4 The Impact of Machine Learning on Various Industries

In recent years, machine learning has spearheaded a revolution across various industries, transforming the way businesses operate and opening up a world of new possibilities. By leveraging the vast potential of algorithms and data, machine learning has become a catalyst for innovation, driving improvements in efficiency, decision-making, and customer satisfaction across sectors. Let's explore some of the significant impacts machine learning has had on various industries.

1. Healthcare Sector:
Machine learning applications in healthcare have been revolutionary, helping medical practitioners in diagnostics, treatment planning, and disease prevention. By analyzing massive datasets and learning patterns, machine learning algorithms can predict patient outcomes, identify potential risks, and assist physicians in providing personalized treatment plans. Furthermore, machine learning has greatly aided in medical imaging, contributing to more accurate and efficient diagnoses.

2. Financial Services Industry:
The financial services sector has witnessed a significant shift due to machine learning. Intelligent algorithms can now analyze large financial datasets in real-time, helping banks identify patterns of fraudulent activities and making transactions more secure. Additionally, machine learning algorithms are employed for credit scoring models, enabling better risk assessment and promoting fair lending practices. Furthermore, in stock trading, algorithms have played a substantial role in automating the decision-making process, leading to quicker and more informed investment choices.

3. Retail and E-commerce:
Machine learning is revolutionizing the retail and e-commerce industry, enhancing customer satisfaction, optimizing supply chain management, and streamlining marketing efforts. By analyzing vast amounts of customer data, machine learning algorithms provide valuable insights into customer preferences and behaviors. This helps retailers personalize product recommendations, accurately forecast demand, and optimize pricing strategies to drive sales. In addition, machine learning helps in fraud detection, targeted advertising, and customer churn prediction, ensuring businesses can effectively cater to their customers' needs.

4. Manufacturing and Logistics:
Machine learning's impact on the manufacturing and logistics sector has been substantial. Machine learning algorithms can analyze production data to identify potential bottlenecks, optimize workflows, and make predictions to prevent equipment failures by detecting anomalies. The integration of machine learning in logistics has led to improved route planning, reduced costs, and enhanced customer satisfaction through accurate delivery time estimations. Additionally, machine learning algorithms are assisting in quality control, boosting efficiency in the manufacturing process.

5. Automotive and Transportation:
The automotive sector constantly benefits from machine learning applications. Self-driving cars rely heavily on machine learning algorithms to interpret sensor data, enabling vehicles to make informed decisions in real-time. What was once a distant dream is now being realized with the help of machine learning, paving the way for safer and more efficient transportation. Machine learning has also proved beneficial in mitigating traffic congestion, optimizing public transportation routes, and improving fleet management in logistics and transportation companies.

6. Energy Sector:
Machine learning has brought significant improvement in the

energy sector, facilitating renewable energy integration, optimizing power grid management, and enhancing energy efficiency. By analyzing historical energy consumption patterns and external influencing factors, machine learning algorithms allow for more accurate forecasts, thus reducing the reliance on traditional power plants and enabling better utilization of renewable energy sources. Additionally, machine learning aids in predictive maintenance of equipment and machinery, reducing unplanned downtime and improving energy production efficiency.

These are just a few examples of how machine learning has impacted various industries. The potential of machine learning remains vast and ever-expanding, constantly introducing innovative solutions and reshaping industries worldwide. As technology continues to advance, individuals and companies who embrace machine learning will likely gain a competitive edge and contribute to a future built upon data-driven decision-making processes.

Chapter 2: Types of Machine Learning

Types of Machine Learning
In the previous chapter, we delved into the fundamentals of machine learning and its significance in today's world. Now, it's time to understand the various types of machine learning techniques that are commonly used. From supervised learning to unsupervised learning, each type of machine learning has its own strengths and limitations. This chapter will provide an in-depth exploration of these techniques and help you determine when to implement each type based on your task or problem.

2. 1 Supervised Learning:
Supervised learning is the most widely used and understood type of machine learning. Encompassed within this approach, the model learns by making predictions based on labeled historical data. Labeled data refers to datasets where each input is associated with its corresponding output. For instance, in a dataset consisting of housing prices, the input would be various features like number of rooms and location, and the corresponding output would be the actual house prices.

2. 1. 1 Classification:
Classification is a subtype of supervised learning that deals with predicting discrete categories or classes. The model learns from labeled data to classify new, unlabeled data points into specific categories. For example, image classification algorithms help us identify whether a given image contains a cat or a dog.

2. 1. 2 Regression:
Regression is another subcategory of supervised learning that deals with predicting continuous values. Regression algorithms analyze relationships between variables to predict a continuous outcome. For instance, predicting the price of a stock based on historical data involves regression.

2.2 Unsupervised Learning:

Unlike supervised learning, unsupervised learning does not rely on labeled data. Instead, it focuses on finding patterns, structures, or relationships within the data on its own. This type of learning is particularly beneficial when we don't have predefined labels or don't know what to look for.

2.2.1 Clustering:

Clustering is a popular technique used within unsupervised learning. It aims to group similar data points together based on their inherent characteristics, without any predefined labels. It finds structures and similarities within the data that may not be initially apparent. It can be used for customer segmentation, anomaly detection, and more.

2.2.2 Dimensionality Reduction:

Dimensionality reduction is another powerful approach in unsupervised learning. It aims to reduce the number of variables or features of a dataset while retaining the most pertinent information. By reducing the complexity, we can improve computational efficiency and eliminate noise or irrelevant data.

2.2.3 Association Rule Learning:

Association rule learning is a technique used to discover relationships between variables in vast datasets, commonly observed in market basket analysis or recommendation systems. It focuses on finding associations, dependencies, or correlations between different items.

2.3 Reinforcement Learning:

Reinforcement learning is a unique type of machine learning that involves an agent interacting with an environment, learning by trial and error feedback. It is widely applied in domains such as robotics, gaming, and autonomous systems. The agent learns to take actions by maximizing a reward signal provided by the environment.

2.4 Semi-Supervised Learning:

Semi-supervised learning lies in between supervised and unsupervised learning. It combines both labeled and unlabeled data to improve the modeling accuracy. Utilizing labeled data allows the model to learn patterns and refine its predictions from the unlabeled data.

2.5 Deep Learning:
Deep learning, a subset of machine learning, focuses on artificial neural networks composed of multiple layers, allowing the model to learn intricate representations of complex patterns. It has gained significant popularity and revolutionized many fields, including image recognition, natural language processing, and speech recognition.

Conclusion:
Understanding the various types of machine learning is essential for choosing the right approach to tackle specific problems. Whether you have labeled data and opt for supervised learning, or explore unsupervised learning to uncover patterns within large datasets, each type has its own unique benefits. Remember, you can even combine different approaches to leverage the strengths of various techniques. The next chapter will delve into the machine learning lifecycle and guide you through the steps of successfully building machine learning models.

2.1 Supervised Learning: Principles and Applications

Supervised learning forms the foundation of machine learning techniques. Contained within this chapter, we will delve into the principles and applications of supervised learning, a powerful approach for creating intelligent systems. Whether you are a beginner enthusiast or an aspiring data scientist, this section will equip you with the necessary knowledge to start leveraging supervised learning in your projects effectively.

2.1.1 Understanding Supervised Learning

Supervised learning leverages labeled datasets to train machine learning models and make predictions or decisions based on observed features. The term "supervised" denotes the process by which the model learns from a given set of labeled examples, comparing its own output with the correct labels. By continually adjusting its parameters based on this feedback, the model aims to generalize its learning to make accurate predictions for unseen data.

In supervised learning, each example in the dataset consists of input data, also known as features, and an associated output label. The input data can take various forms, such as numerical values, textual information, images, or audio. The output labels, on the other hand, can be binary (yes/no), categorical (e.g., classification into multiple classes), or continuous (e.g., predicting a numeric value).

2.1.2 Classification

Classification is a prominent task in supervised learning, where the objective is to assign input data to predefined categories or classes. Imagine that you have a dataset containing images of different animals, along with their corresponding labels (e.g., dog, cat, horse). By training a classification model on this dataset, you can develop a system capable of automatically classifying new unseen images into one of these predefined classes.

There are various algorithms used for classification, including decision trees, support vector machines (SVMs), and neural networks. We will discuss these methods in detail in later chapters.

2.1.3 Regression

Regression, another frequently encountered supervised learning task, involves predicting continuous numerical values based on input features. For instance, you can use regression to estimate the house prices based on features like the number of rooms, the location, and the age of the house.

Popular regression algorithms include linear regression, random forests, and gradient boosting techniques. We will explore these algorithms later on, providing comprehensive explanations and hands-on examples.

2.1.4 Model Evaluation

After training a supervised learning model, it is crucial to evaluate its performance to ensure its effectiveness and to identify areas for improvement. Model evaluation involves assessing metrics such as accuracy, precision, recall, and F1-score, depending on the specific task at hand. However, it's important to note that not all evaluation metrics are suited for every problem; therefore, understanding the domain and objective of your task is essential when choosing appropriate evaluation measures.

We will guide you through the different evaluation techniques, highlighting their pros and cons and demonstrating proper usage in practical scenarios.

2.1.5 Overfitting and Underfitting

Overfitting and underfitting are critical concepts in the realm of supervised learning. When a model is overfit, it has learned the training data too well, leading to poor performance on unseen examples. On the other hand, underfitting occurs when the model fails to capture the patterns within the training data, resulting in poor generalization. Balancing between these two extremes is essential to construct models that perform well on unseen data.

We will discuss strategies to detect and mitigate overfitting and underfitting, such as regularization, cross-validation, and model complexity tuning. These techniques will contribute to building robust and reliable models.

2.1.6 Practical Applications

Supervised learning finds applications in various fields and industries. From medical diagnosis and fraud detection to recommendation systems and natural language processing, the possibilities are wide-ranging. Throughout this book, we will include practical examples and case studies, illustrating how supervised learning techniques have been successfully employed to address real-world problems.

We hope this chapter has provided you with a comprehensive introduction to supervised learning and its practical applications. Understanding the core principles and methodologies sets the stage for exploring more advanced concepts in subsequent chapters, as we unlock the vast potential of machine learning.

2.2 Unsupervised Learning: Clustering and Association

In the realm of machine learning, there exist broadly two categories of learning – supervised and unsupervised learning. While supervised learning requires labeled data to train a model, unsupervised learning deals with unlabeled data, making it an exciting and powerful domain to explore. Amid these chapter, we will delve into one of the key aspects of unsupervised learning, specifically clustering and association.

2.2.1 Clustering: Grouping Similar Instances

Clustering is a fundamental technique in unsupervised learning that involves the categorization of data into groups, also known as clusters, based on their similarity. The aim is to create meaningful and distinguishable clusters that capture the inherent patterns or structures within the data. This allows us to uncover relationships and gain valuable insights into the data without having any prior knowledge or target variable.

The most popular approach to clustering is the K-means algorithm. This algorithm partitiones the data into K distinct clusters, where K is a pre-defined number chosen by the practitioner. The process starts by randomly initializing K cluster centroids. Subsequently, it iteratively assigns each data point to the nearest centroid and recalculates the centroid positions based on the updated assignments. This process continues until the centroids no longer change significantly or a termination criterion is met. The final result is K distinct clusters, each containing data points that are similar to one another, but different from those in other clusters.

Another notable clustering algorithm is hierarchical clustering.

Unlike K-means, it does not require specifying the number of desired clusters in advance. It organizes data points into a hierarchy of nested clusters, forming a tree-like structure known as a dendrogram. We can then choose to cut this dendrogram at different heights to obtain different numbers of clusters. This method provides a richer view of the data, allowing us to explore multiple levels of details within the clusters.

2.2.2 Association: Discovering Patterns and Co-occurrences

Association is another important concept within unsupervised learning, which seeks to identify interesting associations or relationships between variables in a dataset. Its primary goal is to unearth patterns of co-occurrence or item dependencies that can be leveraged for recommendation systems or market basket analysis, among other applications.

The most well-known algorithm for association rule mining is the Apriori algorithm. It is based on the idea that if an itemset is frequent, then all of its subsets must also be frequent. The algorithm scans the dataset multiple times, slowly building up a set of frequent itemsets, also known as large itemsets. It starts by identifying all single items as large itemsets and then combines them to generate larger and more complex itemsets. Eventually, it finds all the significant itemsets that meet the minimum support and confidence thresholds specified by the user.

Association rule mining output consists of rules that follow a specific notation, typically expressed as "if X, then Y". X and Y represent antecedents and consequents, respectively. These rules capture dependencies between items or combinations of items, which can be incredibly helpful in making recommendations or understanding how certain items tend to co-occur.

Both clustering and association techniques are powerful in different contexts. Clustering helps us organizationally understand the data by grouping similar instances, while association rules enable us to identify patterns and co-occurrences beneficial in various domains. By harnessing these methods, one can gain valuable insights into the underlying structure and behavior of unlabeled data.

Remember, proper preprocessing and data exploration are crucial when applying unsupervised learning techniques. Carefully considering the nature of your data and selecting appropriate algorithms will help you tackle real-world problems and gain actionable knowledge from unlabelled datasets.

2.3 Reinforcement Learning: Fundamentals and Realworld Scenarios

2.3 Reinforcement Learning: Fundamentals and Real-world Scenarios

Amidst the information in this section, we will delve into the intriguing concept of reinforcement learning (RL). It is a branch of machine learning that focuses on teaching an agent to make a sequence of decisions, optimizing its actions based on rewards obtained from interacting with an environment. This powerful technique has achieved remarkable success in various real-world scenarios, making it an essential tool for any aspiring machine learning practitioner.

Fundamentals of Reinforcement Learning:
Reinforcement learning revolves around the notion of an agent learning from trial and error through interaction with an environment. Unlike other machine learning branches that rely on labeled input-output pairs, RL agents receive feedback in the form of rewards or penalties that guide their learning process.

The core elements of reinforcement learning can be summed up as follows:

1. Agent: The learning entity responsible for taking actions. It observes the environment and decides upon actions to maximize rewards.

2. Environment: The external system within which the agent operates. It responds to the actions chosen by the agent and provides rewards based on the outcome.

3. Actions: The decisions taken by the agent after observing the environment state. These actions affect the agent's next state and subsequent rewards.

4. State: The representation of the environment at any given point in time. It is the agent's perception of the system and is essential for decision-making.

5. Rewards: The feedback signals that the agent receives after taking actions in the environment. Rewards can be positive, negative, or neutral, and they guide the learning process.

Reinforcement learning algorithms are designed to find the optimal policy, a strategy that maximizes long-term rewards for the agent. The policy can be deterministic, where each state leads to an explicit action, or stochastic, where probabilities of actions are determined.

Real-world Applications:
Reinforcement learning has proven to be incredibly versatile, leading to successes in numerous real-world scenarios. Let's explore some practical examples where RL has been applied:

1. Game Playing: Reinforcement learning became widely recognized when AlphaGo, an RL-powered program, achieved significant success against world-renowned Go players. RL enables game-playing agents to learn optimal strategies by repeatedly playing against themselves or human players.

2. Robotics: Reinforcement learning plays a crucial role in training robotic systems. By providing rewards and penalizing undesirable behaviors during training, robots can learn to perform complex tasks such as grasping objects or navigating through unknown environments.

3. Autonomous Vehicles: Autonomous driving relies heavily on reinforcement learning principles. Agents are trained to make quick and safe decisions based on their environment

observations, allowing vehicles to navigate traffic, make lane changes, and even avoid accidents.

4. Energy Management: With the increasing demand for energy-efficient systems, reinforcement learning is being employed to optimize energy usage. Agents can learn to adjust energy-consuming devices such as heating, ventilation, and air conditioning (HVAC) systems to minimize power consumption while maintaining user comfort.

5. Financial Systems: Reinforcement learning has found valuable applications in finance. Agents can learn to make investment decisions, optimize trading strategies, and emulate the behavior of an expert trader.

The promises of reinforcement learning extend far beyond these examples. With its ability to enable agents to make decisions in uncertain, dynamic environments, RL has the potential to revolutionize numerous fields, from healthcare to cybersecurity.

Getting Started:
Embarking on your journey with reinforcement learning can be exhilarating yet challenging. Here's a step-by-step guideline to help you get started:

1. Familiarize yourself with the mathematical foundations behind RL, including Markov Decision Processes (MDPs), value functions, and policy optimization.

2. Gain practical experience by implementing simple RL algorithms such as Q-Learning and Monte Carlo methods. Understand how these algorithms interact with an environment, learn from rewards, and modify their behavior accordingly.

3. Dive deeper into more advanced algorithms like Deep Q-Networks (DQN), Proximal Policy Optimization (PPO), and Trust Region Policy Optimization (TRPO). Explore their strengths, weaknesses, and real-world applications.

4. Experiment with RL frameworks such as OpenAI Gym, TensorFlow, or PyTorch to gain hands-on experience with realistic simulations and complex environments.

5. Stay up to date with the latest research papers, attend conferences, and participate in RL competitions to hone your skills and stay ahead of the curve.

Reinforcement learning is a journey of understanding the art of decision-making in complex and uncertain scenarios. As you persist and explore the depths of RL, you will witness its transformative potential and be inspired to create intelligent systems capable of adapting and learning from their environment.

Good luck and enjoy the exciting world of reinforcement learning!

2.4 Hybrid Learning Approaches and Choosing the Right Model

Machine learning models come in various forms, each with its strengths and weaknesses. To overcome the limitations and maximize the potential of machine learning algorithms, hybrid learning approaches have emerged as a powerful solution. Amid these section, we will explore hybrid learning approaches and guide you in choosing the right model for your specific problem.

Hybrid learning refers to combining multiple machine learning techniques or models to achieve enhanced prediction and decision-making capabilities. By leveraging the strengths of different models, a hybrid approach can compensate for the weaknesses of individual algorithms, leading to increased accuracy and efficiency.

There are several reasons to adopt hybrid learning instead of relying only on a single machine learning model. First, different models have varying abilities to represent complex patterns, capture various data characteristics, or generalize the learned information. By combining diverse models, hybrid learning can leverage their complementary strengths to handle a wide range of data scenarios effectively.

Hybrid learning also offers a solution when the relationship between data features and the output is nonlinear or uncertain. In such cases, linear models may fall short in capturing intricate interactions between variables. By incorporating nonlinear models like neural networks or decision trees, hybrid learning can capture complex relationships that exist in the data.

When selecting the appropriate hybrid learning method, it is crucial to consider the nature of the problem, available data, and desired learning outcome. Let's discuss some popular hybrid learning approaches and their applications.

1. Ensemble Learning:
Ensemble learning combines multiple models, developed independently, to form a more robust and accurate predictor. Popular ensemble techniques include Random Forest, Gradient Boosting, AdaBoost, and Stacking. Ensemble learning is particularly effective when working with datasets containing high levels of noise, outliers, or missing values.

2. Transfer Learning:
Transfer learning allows the knowledge learned from one domain or task to be applied effectively in another. Instead of training a model from scratch for a specific problem, transfer learning involves leveraging pre-trained models and adapting them to the new task. This approach is practical when there is limited data available for a particular problem or when training a model from scratch may be time-consuming.

3. Reinforcement Learning with Deep Learning:
This hybrid approach combines the power of reinforcement learning algorithms with deep neural networks. Reinforcement learning focuses on selecting actions to maximize rewards in an environment. When combined with deep learning, this approach has proven to be highly effective in areas such as game playing, robotics, and autonomous driving.

4. Hybrid Generative-Discriminative Modeling:
This approach combines generative models, which capture the detailed structure of a dataset, with discriminative models, which focus on classifying or predicting specific outputs. By merging these two types of models, hybrid generative-discriminative approaches can provide a sharper understanding of complex distribution structures and improve prediction performance. Gaussian Mixture Models (GMM) combined with Support Vector Machines (SVM) is an example of such an approach.

Before choosing a hybrid learning approach, consider the trade-offs in terms of computational complexity, scalability, and interpretability. Analyze the data for which the model is intended, the availability of computational resources, and the interpretability requirements of the applications. Also, keep in mind that hybrid learning may require additional expertise and time for implementation and fine-tuning.

To select the most suitable hybrid learning model, follow these steps:
1. Understand your problem: Clearly define the problem statement and identify what kind of relationship you seek between input features and outputs.
2. Explore the data: Examine the characteristics, size, and distribution of available data. This knowledge will assist in identifying appropriate models that can handle the specific data attributes.
3. Analyze model requirements: Based on the data analysis, choose models that align with your problem requirements, such as capturing complex relationships, handling outliers, scalability, or interpretability needs.
4. Experiment and compare: Implement multiple hybrid learning approaches using your chosen models and evaluate their performances. Use appropriate evaluation metrics to measure accuracy, precision, recall, or other criteria specific to your problem domain.
5. Fine-tune and validate: Adjust the hyperparameters, evaluate the optimal settings, and validate the results on unseen data (testing set).
6. Document lessons learned: Record insights gained during the process, including challenges encountered, effective techniques, and learnings derived from experimentation. These records can be invaluable for future projects and research endeavors.

Remember, hybrid learning approaches require continuous learning and adaptation. As you progress further and gain more experience, you may discover new combinations or variations that can further improve your models' performance.

In conclusion, hybrid learning approaches integrate the strengths of multiple models to enhance the accuracy and efficiency of predictions. Ensemble learning, transfer learning, reinforcement learning with deep learning, and hybrid generative-discriminative modeling are some popular techniques in hybrid learning. By considering the problem at hand, available data, and desired learning outcome, you can select the most appropriate hybrid learning model and iteratively optimize it for your specific needs.

Chapter 3: Data Exploration and Preprocessing

Data Exploration and Preprocessing

Amidst the pages of this chapter, we will delve into the crucial aspects of data exploration and preprocessing in machine learning. Before diving into the intricacies of building and training models, it is vital to develop a deep understanding of the raw data that will be used for analysis. It is through the process of data exploration and preprocessing that we can gain insights, uncover patterns, and ready our data for further analysis.

3. 1 Understanding Data:

Before we can begin exploring our data, it is pivotal to know the nature of the dataset we are working with. Data comes in various forms, such as numerical, categorical, or textual. Each type of data necessitates different preprocessing techniques. Numerical data can be continuous or discrete, while categorical data can be nominal or ordinal.

Data exploration begins with a thorough examination of the dataset's structure, size, and distributions to gain a perspective on its characteristics. One can investigate features, also known as variables, and their potential relationships. Visualization techniques like histograms, scatter plots, and pair plots help us comprehend the data better.

3. 2 Handling Missing Data:

One crucial challenge in working with real-world data is the existence of missing values. Incomplete or missing data can significantly affect the performance of any machine learning algorithm. There are several techniques to deal with missing data, including deletion, mean or median imputation, hot-deck imputation, and advanced techniques like multiple imputation. The choice of method depends on the data at hand and the underlying assumption of missingness.

3. 3 Dealing with Outliers:

Outliers are observations that deviate significantly from the overall pattern of the data. These anomalies, if left unaddressed, can bias the machine learning models or misrepresent the true trends and patterns in the data. Various techniques, such as statistical tests, box plots, or clustering algorithms, can identify and handle outliers effectively. Outliers can be treated through methods like trimming, winsorization, or replacing them with imputed values.

3. 4 Feature Scaling:

Machine learning models often require feature scaling to ensure that all features contribute equally to the analysis and that no particular feature dominates the others due to its magnitude. Common feature scaling techniques include standardization and normalization. Standardization transforms the data distribution to have zero mean and unit variance, accommodating machine learning models relying on assumptions of normality. Normalization scales the data to a specific range, often between 0 and 1. Choosing an appropriate scaling technique depends on the nature and requirements of your data.

3. 5 Encoding Categorical Variables:

Categorical variables pose a unique challenge during data preprocessing as machine learning models generally require numerical inputs. Two common methods to encode categorical variables include label encoding and one-hot encoding. Label encoding assigns a unique integer value to each unique category, while one-hot encoding creates binary features for each category. The choice between these methods depends on the number of categories and their relationships within the dataset.

3. 6 Feature Transformation:

Sometimes, the raw data provided might not be suitable for modeling due to reasons like skewed distributions or nonlinear relationships. In such cases, feature transformation becomes necessary. Techniques such as log transformation, power transformation, or polynomial expansion can help improve the distributional properties of data and establish meaningful relationships between features.

3. 7 Dimensionality Reduction:

In situations where the dataset includes a large number of features, dimensionality reduction techniques become essential. These techniques aim to simplify the data representation while preserving the most crucial aspects. Principal Component Analysis (PCA) and Singular Value Decomposition (SVD) are commonly used techniques for dimensionality reduction. By reducing the number of features, these methods help with computational efficiency and alleviate the risk of overfitting.

Conclusion:

Data exploration and preprocessing lay the groundwork for subsequent stages of the machine learning pipeline. Through careful examination, handling of missing data, addressing outliers, scaling features, encoding categorical variables, performing feature transformations, and ultimately reducing dimensionality if needed, we can unlock the full potential of our data. An effective preprocessing pipeline empowers us to build accurate and robust models, ultimately leading to valuable insights and predictions.

3.1 The Role of Data in Machine Learning

Machine learning is a subsection of artificial intelligence that revolves around creating systems and algorithms that can learn and improve from data instead of being explicitly programmed. Embraced by this chapter, we will delve into the significant role that data plays in machine learning and how it forms the foundation upon which these algorithms operate and improve.

At its core, machine learning thrives on the availability of vast amounts of data. Data can be thought of as the fuel that powers the engine of machine learning algorithms. These algorithms take in data, analyze it, find patterns, and use these patterns to make predictions, decisions, or gain new insights. The more diverse and representative the data are, the better the algorithms can perform.

Let's start by understanding the two primary types of data used in machine learning: labeled and unlabeled data.

Labeled data refers to data instances where each sample is accompanied by a predefined label that represents the ground truth or the expected output. In other words, for a machine learning algorithm to learn from labeled data, human experts must manually annotate the samples. For instance, in a supervised learning setting, where the algorithm requires guidance to learn, labeled data serves as a benchmark to study patterns and make accurate predictions.

Consider a scenario where we need to build a spam email classifier. The algorithm, during the training phase, would require a labeled dataset containing emails delineated as either spam or legitimate. With these labels, the algorithm can analyze the patterns, language use, email structure, or other relevant features to classify future emails accurately.

Unlabeled data, on the other hand, consists of data instances without any predefined labels or ground truth. The absence of labels in these datasets poses a more challenging task for machine learning algorithms. However, unlabeled data is abundant and relatively easy to obtain, as no human expertise or manual labeling is required.

Unsupervised learning algorithms tackle the problem of analyzing and finding interesting patterns or structures within unlabeled data. These algorithms discover underlying trends, grouping tendencies, or latent factors that may not be apparent to the human eye. Clustering and dimensionality reduction techniques are used extensively in unsupervised learning to classify similar data points, identify outliers, or visualize complex datasets.

In recent years, the emphasis on utilizing both labeled and unlabeled data has led to the development of semi-supervised learning algorithms. These algorithms take advantage of the larger pool of unlabeled data and a smaller set of labeled data to improve performance. By propagating information from labeled to unlabeled data, these algorithms can make more accurate predictions and decision-making.

Now that we understand the different types of data, it is important to recognize the impact of data quantity and quality on machine learning systems. When it comes to quantity, more data is generally preferred. The size and variety of data enable algorithms to etch more precise decision boundaries or correlations. However, this does not imply that throwing more data at the problem is always beneficial. There is a trade-off between data quantity and the resources consumed in processing and training algorithms.

On the other hand, data quality focuses on the relevancy, accuracy, and bias present within data. Poor data quality can lead to misleading patterns, incorrect predictions, or biased decision-making. It is crucial to perform thorough data cleaning, preprocessing, and validation to mitigate any adverse effects of poor quality data.

Additionally, it is essential to address data bias in machine learning. Any biases, conscious or unconscious, carried by the data collection process, human labeling, or historical patterns, can be directly and inadvertently injected into machine learning algorithms. These biases can lead to unfair or discriminatory results, impacting targeted populations or exacerbating disparities. Regular monitoring and auditing of data inputs are essential steps to mitigate such biases and ensure fairness and inclusivity.

In summary, data plays a fundamental role in machine learning. Labeled data enables supervised learning algorithms to learn patterns and make accurate predictions. Unlabeled data poses challenges but can be powerfully harnessed to identify underlying structures and trends through unsupervised learning algorithms. The combination of labeled and unlabeled data has also led to the advancement of semi-supervised learning. The quantity and quality of data are crucial factors that should be considered while building machine learning systems. Proper preparation and cleansing of data, as well as addressing biases, are vital to ensure effective and responsible machine learning applications.

3.2 Exploratory Data Analysis (EDA) Techniques

Exploratory Data Analysis (EDA) Techniques

Exploratory Data Analysis (EDA) is an essential step in the machine learning pipeline. It involves inspecting, cleaning, and analyzing data to uncover patterns, trends, and relationships. By utilizing various EDA techniques, you can gain valuable insights into your dataset, identify potential issues, and make informed decisions for subsequent machine learning tasks. Entailed within this section, we will explore several valuable EDA techniques that will help you explore, understand, and prepare your data effectively.

1. Data Visualization:
One of the most powerful EDA techniques is visually representing the data through plots and charts. Visualization allows you to grasp the distribution, patterns, and anomalies in the dataset. Commonly used visualizations include histograms, scatter plots, bar charts, box plots, and heat maps. Histograms help understand the distribution of numerical variables, scatter plots show relationships between two variables, bar charts display categorical data, while box plots summarize the overall distribution of a variable. Heat maps, on the other hand, provide a visual representation of associations or correlations between variables.

2. Summary Statistics:
Another vital EDA technique is obtaining summary statistics that provide a concise overview of the dataset. Measures such as mean, median, mode, range, variance, and standard deviation provide insights into the central tendency, spread, and overall distribution of numerical variables. Summary statistics help

identify potential outliers, skewed distributions, and abnormal patterns within the data.

3. Missing Data Handling:
As datasets often contain missing values, it is crucial to address this issue during EDA. Take note of the missing data percentage in each variable and decide how to handle it. Various strategies include imputation, removing rows or columns with missing data, or creating a separate category for missing values if dealing with categorical data. Understanding the distribution and patterns of missing values helps prevent biased interpretations downstream.

4. Outlier Detection:
Outliers are data points that deviate significantly from the majority and may affect subsequent analysis. EDA techniques like box plots, scatter plots, and z-score calculations aid in identifying outliers. It is essential to explore whether outliers are due to measurement errors, data corruption, or represent truly unique samples. Deciding on the appropriate treatment for outliers, such as removal, transformation, or imputation, depends on domain knowledge and the objectives of your machine learning task.

5. Correlation Analysis:
EDA allows you to explore the relationships between variables. Correlation analysis measures the strength and direction of the linear relationship between two numerical variables. Scatter plots and correlation coefficients (e.g., Pearson's or Spearman's) assist in understanding and visualizing these correlations. Identifying highly correlated features can help in feature selection and reducing dimensionality, while also uncovering potential multicollinearity issues that may affect model performance.

6. Feature Engineering:
EDA plays a crucial role in feature engineering, which involves creating new features from existing ones to improve model performance. Understanding the data distribution and

relationships can guide you towards generating insightful features. For example, you can engineer interaction terms, polynomial features, or derive categorical features from numerical ones. Feature engineering can have a significant impact on model predictive power and EDA helps in making informed decisions about which features to engineer or exclude.

7. Time Series Analysis:
When working with time-dependent data, time series analysis during EDA helps detect patterns and trends over time. Techniques such as line plots, autocorrelation plots, and decomposition methods (e.g., seasonal decomposition of time series or moving averages) help reveal seasonal patterns, trends, and potential outliers in time series data. Understanding such patterns is vital for forecasting, anomaly detection, or identifying cyclical variations within your dataset.

In conclusion, Exploratory Data Analysis (EDA) forms a critical part of the machine learning workflow. By leveraging various EDA techniques like data visualization, summary statistics, missing data handling, outlier detection, correlation analysis, feature engineering, and time series analysis, you can gain an in-depth understanding of your dataset. EDA enables you to identify data quirks, clean the dataset, create meaningful features, and make informed decisions for subsequent steps within the machine learning pipeline.

3.3 Data Cleaning and Handling Missing Values

In any machine learning project, data quality plays a crucial role in determining the performance and accuracy of your models. Data cleaning is an essential step that helps eliminate errors, outliers, and inconsistencies, ensuring that your dataset is reliable and suitable for analysis. One common issue often encountered during this data cleaning process is handling missing values.

Missing values can occur in datasets for various reasons, such as human errors during data entry, sensor malfunctions, or simply that the data was not collected for a particular observation. However, having missing values can significantly impact your analysis and machine learning models if not addressed properly. Amidst the pages of this section, we will explore multiple techniques and strategies to identify, handle, and resolve missing values effectively.

1. Identifying Missing Values:
Before diving into handling missing values, let's explore several common representations of missing values that you might encounter in your dataset:
- Blank or empty fields.
- NaN (Not a Number) value, commonly found in numeric datasets.
- Placeholder values like "N/A" or "Not available."
- Zero values that might indicate missing information in certain contexts.

It is vital to identify these missing values because they might behave differently during analysis or modeling, and improperly handling them might lead to biased or inaccurate results.

2. Missing Data Exploration:
To understand the impact of missing values, it is crucial to examine the dataset more comprehensively. Start by observing the presence and patterns of missing values across variables. Determine if the missingness is random, systematic, or missing in specific patterns. By analyzing missing data, you can gain insight into potential factors that might have contributed to missing values.

3. Handling Missing Values:
Now, let's explore different techniques for handling missing values:

3.1. Deleting Rows:
The simplest approach to handle missing values is to remove rows that contain missing entries or a significant number of missing values. However, this approach should be used judiciously, as it might result in data loss and could greatly impact the quality or coherence of your dataset.

3.2. Deleting Columns:
Similar to deleting rows, you can also remove entire columns that have a high percentage of missing values, particularly when those columns provide no valuable or essential information for your analysis or modeling.

3.3. Fill Interpolation:
One popular approach is filling missing values by interpolation. Interpolation estimates missing values based on the available neighboring observations. This approach works exceptionally well for time-series or sequential data, as you can estimate missing values based on trends, periodicity, or other patterns.

3.4. Fill Values Based on Data Characteristics:
For numerical data, you can choose to fill in missing values with mean, median, or mode values of the respective features. This approach assumes that the missing values are missing at random (MAR) and filling them with typical measures would not

introduce significant bias.

3.5. Advanced Algorithms:
Alternatively, you can employ more advanced algorithms like regression models, machine learning models, or matrix factorization methods to predict missing values based on the relationship between the target variable and the other features. These methods can be advantageous when there are complex dependencies between variables and patterns in missing values following certain rules.

3.6. Indicator Method:
Sometimes, missing values themselves can be informative and trying to fill them might lead to loss of critical information. In such cases, you can add an additional binary indicator variable to indicate whether a specific value was missing or not. This indicator variable can be useful in cases where the fact of missingness itself holds valuable information for the analysis or modeling tasks.

4. Iterative Methods:
In more sophisticated scenarios, multiple approaches can be combined in an iterative manner. Multiple imputation techniques such as MICE (Multivariate Imputation by Chained Equations) can be utilized to enhance the accuracy and comprehensiveness of handling missing values. MICE algorithm estimates missing values by creating several imputations based on regression or random forest models, capturing the underlying pattern and reducing potential bias.

Handling missing values adequately is crucial for maintaining data integrity and ensuring robust and unbiased analyses. By understanding the different techniques and utilizing them appropriately, you will be prepared to handle missing values in your datasets effectively and extract meaningful insights for your machine learning projects.

3.4 Feature Engineering: Optimizing Data for Models

When it comes to building machine learning models, having appropriate features is crucial for achieving accurate and reliable predictions. Feature engineering is the process of transforming raw data into suitable forms that effectively represent the underlying patterns and relationships in the data. This chapter will delve into the realm of feature engineering, exploring various techniques and considerations for optimizing data for models.

3.4.1 Understanding the Role of Features

Features, also referred to as input variables or independent variables, are the building blocks that facilitate a machine learning model's ability to generalize from data and make accurate predictions. In a simplistic view, features can be seen as dimensions along which data points can be compared.

When selecting features, it is essential to choose those that possess the most meaningful information relevant to the problem at hand. This selection process involves domain knowledge and an understanding of the problem domain, as well as exploration of the available data. Understanding how different features impact an outcome is crucial for effectively modeling and leveraging them.

3.4.2 Feature Types and Representation

Features can take various forms, and their representation depends on the type of data being used. There are three main types of features:

1. Numerical Features: These features represent quantitative data. Examples include age, income, temperature, or any value that can be expressed with numbers. Numerical features can be further categorized into discrete (countable, e.g., number of pets) or continuous (measurable, e.g., weight). It is important to appropriately scale numerical features to prevent any dominance issues during model training.

2. Categorical Features: These features represent qualitative data with distinct categories. Examples include gender, color, or any attribute that falls into distinct classes. Categorical features can be one-hot encoded, transforming them into multiple binary columns, where each class is represented by a 1 if it applies to a particular data point, otherwise 0.

3. Textual Features: These features involve unstructured text data, like reviews, tweets, or articles. Textual features usually require additional preprocessing steps to convert them into a numerical representation. Popular techniques for dealing with textual features include bag-of-words, word embeddings, and vectorization via methods like Term Frequency-Inverse Document Frequency (TF-IDF) or Word2Vec.

It is fundamental to ensure that the chosen representation takes into account the unique characteristics of the feature type and aligns with the model's requirements.

3.4.3 Handling Missing Data

Data in real-world scenarios is rarely perfect, and missing values pose challenges to the effectiveness of machine learning models. It is a common practice to either impute or remove missing values to avoid bias or incorrect results during training and inference phases.

For numerical features, common techniques for handling

missing data involve imputation by mean, median, or using more advanced methods like K-Nearest Neighbors (k-NN) or regression-based imputation. For categorical features, missing values can be safely introduced as a separate category, which enables the model to distinguish them from real observations. Alternatively, for categorical features with low missing values, removing rows with missing values is a viable option.

3.4.4 Scaling and Normalization

Scaling and normalization are preprocessing steps often necessary when features are in different ranges or units. This practice is vital to bring all features to a common scale, which can streamline model convergence and improve performance. Variations in scales among features might influence models with distance or gradient-based learning algorithms.

Common scaling techniques include min-max scaling, where feature values are transformed to a given range (e.g., [0, 1]), and standardization, which transforms the features such that they have zero mean and unit variance. The choice of scaling technique depends on the underlying distribution of the data and the modeling task itself.

3.4.5 Feature Creation and Extraction

Feature creation involves combining existing features or applying mathematical functions on them to derive new, potentially more informative features. Domain knowledge plays a key role in this process, as novel feature creation reduces the reliance on the raw data representation.

Feature extraction is another technique for generating new features, particularly useful when working with high-dimensional data or unstructured data like images. Common techniques for feature extraction include Principal Component Analysis (PCA) or deep learning-based approaches like

Convolutional Neural Networks (CNNs) for extracting relevant features from images. By reducing the dimensionality or encoding essential patterns, feature extraction can improve both training efficiency and model generalization.

3.4.6 Handling Nonlinearities and Interactions

In certain cases, the relationship between features and the output may exhibit nonlinear behavior or contain complex interactions. As linear models might struggle to capture this complexity by design, feature engineering can aid in addressing these shortcomings.

Polynomial feature augmentation is a technique that incorporates programmatic feature engineering by generating transformation products from the original features. By including higher-order terms or interaction terms, the model gains the ability to capture nonlinear relationships and complex feature interactions. It is worth noting that while this technique can handle some levels of nonlinearity, deeper models, such as neural networks, may be more appropriate for highly complex tasks.

3.4.7 Removing Redundancy or Collinearity

Redundant or collinear features—those that offer very similar or indistinguishable information—can negatively affect model performance, increase computation time, and introduce overfitting risks. Detecting and removing such features is crucial to avoid unnecessary complexity and ensure model robustness.

Methods like correlation analysis can help assess the pairwise relationship between features. In cases of high correlation, one of the features can be dropped or replaced with a derived feature that preserves the relevant information. Other dimensionality reduction techniques, such as L1 or L2 regularization, can also be applied to achieve feature selection, reducing the risk of overfitting.

3.4.8 Handling Time-Series Features

In time-series analysis, observations are generally ordered by time, and features can exploit additional temporal dependencies or trends contained within the data. Techniques like lag features allow models to incorporate previous time steps' historical information, capturing relationships across different points in time.

While feature engineering solely for time-series analysis is an extensive topic, adding time-related statistics, trends, or seasonality components as additional features can enhance model performance and forecasting capabilities.

Conclusion

Feature engineering plays an essential role in optimizing data for machine learning models. The correct treatment and manipulation of features increase model sensitivity, helps avoid bias and overfitting, and captures the underlying patterns in the data. Employing appropriate techniques for feature selection, transformation, imputation, scaling, and handling nonlinearities significantly impacts model performance. Remember, always partner domain expertise with an exploration of available techniques to unlock the true potential of feature engineering for your machine learning projects.

Chapter 4: Model Development and Training

Model Development and Training

In the previous chapters, we have explored the foundations and essential concepts of machine learning. Now, we will delve into the exciting world of model development and training. This is where the real magic happens—where data transforms into meaningful insights and predictions. Engulfed by this chapter, we will discuss the various steps involved in the model development process, from data preparation to fine-tuning.

4.1 Data Preparation:
Before embarking upon model development, it is crucial to prepare and preprocess the data that will be used for training. This stage involves cleaning the data, handling missing values, normalizing or standardizing features, and splitting the data into training and testing sets. Data preparation plays a vital role in the performance of the final model, as using raw or unclean data can severely affect its accuracy and efficacy.

4.2 Feature Engineering:
Feature engineering refers to the process of selecting, transforming, and creating meaningful features from the available data. It involves identifying relevant variables, combining related features, and creating new features to enhance the predictive power of the model. Feature engineering is both an art and a science, requiring a deep understanding of the problem domain and intuition to extract valuable insights hidden in the data.

4.3 Model Selection:
The choice of an appropriate machine learning model greatly

impacts the performance of the final solution. There are numerous algorithms to choose from, each with its own strengths and weaknesses. Decision trees, regression models, support vector machines, random forests, and neural networks are some popular models. Model selection should be based on the nature of the problem, the size of the dataset, and the desired level of accuracy.

4.4 Model Training:
Once the data is ready and the model selected, it's time to train the model. Training involves fitting the model to the training dataset, allowing it to learn patterns and relationships between the input features and the target variable. During the training process, the model optimizes its internal parameters to minimize the difference between predicted outputs and actual values. Different training algorithms are used, such as gradient descent, to update model parameters iteratively.

4.5 Hyperparameter Tuning:
Models have hyperparameters that control their behavior during training. These parameters, such as learning rate, regularization strength, or the number of hidden layers in a neural network, are not learned from the data but set by the user beforehand. To optimize model performance, hyperparameter tuning is required, which involves systematically exploring different combinations of hyperparameters and evaluating their impact on the model's performance.

4.6 Evaluation Metrics:
After training the model, it is crucial to evaluate its performance. Common evaluation metrics depend on the nature of the problem at hand. For classification tasks, metrics like accuracy, precision, recall, and F1 score are commonly used. Whereas, for regression problems, metrics like mean squared error, mean absolute error, and R-squared are the go-to choices. Evaluation metrics help assess the model's predictive power and guide further improvements if needed.

4.7 Regularization:

Overfitting is a common challenge in machine learning, where the model becomes too specialized on the training data and fails to generalize well on unseen data. Regularization techniques, such as L1 and L2 regularization, dropout, or early stopping, can help mitigate overfitting. Regularization adds additional constraints to the model's training process, preventing it from becoming overly complex and improving its generalization capabilities.

4.8 Model Deployment:
Once the model is trained and evaluated, it is ready for deployment. This involves integrating the model into a production environment where it can make predictions on new, unseen data. Various deployment options exist, such as hosting the model on cloud platforms, embedding it into mobile applications, or deploying it locally in a server. Model performance should be monitored over time to ensure its accuracy and reliability in real-world scenarios.

Engulfed by this chapter, we have covered the essential steps of model development and training. From data preparation to selecting the right model, training, hyperparameter tuning, and evaluation, each step is crucial for building accurate and effective machine learning models. The journey doesn't end here—further fine-tuning and continuous assessment of the model's performance will be essential to ensure its success in practical applications. With this knowledge in hand, you are now equipped to venture deeper into the realm of machine learning and unleash its power to transform and innovate across various domains.

4.1 Overview of Model Building

Building a model is a fundamental aspect of machine learning. It involves creating a mathematical representation that can provide predictions, classifications, or insights based on input data. Within the context of this section, we will provide an overview of the model building process to help you understand how machine learning algorithms work.

4.1.1 Problem Definition
Before embarking on the model building journey, it is crucial to clearly define the problem you are trying to solve. Are you aiming to predict future sales, classify images, or analyze customer behavior? By defining the problem, you can determine the type of model to build and the appropriate algorithm to use.

4.1.2 Data Collection and Preparation
Once the problem is defined, the next step is to gather the necessary data. This involves identifying relevant datasets and ensuring their availability. You may need to collect data manually, extract it from existing databases, or use publicly available datasets.

After gathering the data, you must carefully prepare it for analysis. This includes cleaning the data by removing errors, handling missing values, and dealing with outliers. Additionally, data preprocessing techniques such as normalization and feature scaling may be required to ensure the data is in a suitable format for the model.

4.1.3 Feature Selection and Engineering
Feature selection and engineering refer to the process of selecting the most relevant features from the available data and creating new features that enhance the predictive power of the model. This step aims to reduce the dimensionality of the dataset

and focus on the features that have the most impact on the target variable.

Feature selection techniques include statistical methods, such as correlation analysis and recursive feature elimination, which assess the importance of each feature. Feature engineering involves creating new features based on domain knowledge, data transformations, or generating interaction terms to capture complex relationships.

4.1.4 Choosing the Algorithm

The choice of algorithm depends on the problem type (e.g., regression, classification) and the characteristics of the data. For example, linear regression, support vector machines, decision trees, and neural networks are popular algorithms used for different types of problems.

Considerations when choosing an algorithm include its complexity, interpretability, performance on similar problems, and scalability. It is recommended to start with simpler algorithms and gradually progress to more complex ones as needed.

4.1.5 Model Training and Evaluation

After selecting an algorithm, the next step is to train the model using the prepared data. This involves minimizing an objective function that quantifies the difference between the predicted and actual values (or labels). The training process adjusts the model's internal parameters to find the best fit for the training data.

Once trained, the model needs to be evaluated to estimate its performance and generalization ability. Performance metrics such as accuracy, precision, recall, and F1 score are commonly used to assess the model's effectiveness. Cross-validation techniques help validate the model on unseen data to check for overfitting.

4.1.6 Model Optimization and Fine-tuning

The initial model may not always deliver the best possible

performance. Optimization techniques, such as tweaking hyperparameters or regularizing the model, can improve its generalization capabilities. Hyperparameter tuning involves selecting the right values for parameters that are not learned during training. This is typically done through grid search or random search to find the best combination.

Fine-tuning may also involve adjusting the model's architecture, adding regularization techniques, or employing ensemble methods. The aim is to strike a balance between model complexity and capacity to capture patterns in the data.

4.1.7 Deployment and Monitoring

Once the model is optimized and fine-tuned, it can be deployed in a real-world application. This may involve integrating it into an existing system or building a new system around it. It is essential to monitor the model's performance and retrain it periodically to adapt to changing data patterns.

Regular monitoring of the model's predictions, input data distribution, and feedback from users is crucial to ensure its continued effectiveness. Continuous improvement and adaptation are key when deploying machine learning models in dynamic environments.

In conclusion, building a machine learning model involves defining the problem, collecting and preparing the data, selecting relevant features, choosing an appropriate algorithm, training and evaluating the model, optimizing its performance, and finally deploying it for real-world use. By following this general overview, you can start your journey into the exciting field of machine learning.

4.2 Algorithm Selection and Model Architecture

In the vast field of machine learning, one crucial aspect is algorithm selection and model architecture. This step heavily influences the predictive power and performance of a machine learning model. Whether you are solving a classification, regression, or clustering problem, selecting appropriate algorithms and designing an ideal model architecture can significantly impact the accuracy and efficiency of your solution. Housed within this section, we will explore algorithm selection and model architecture in detail.

4.2.1 Algorithm Selection:
Choosing the right algorithm is paramount to the success of your machine learning project. Each algorithm possesses different strengths and is suitable for specific types of problems. To begin, it is important to understand the fundamental algorithm categories and their applications:

1. Supervised Learning Algorithms: These algorithms are used when we have pre-labeled training data and aim to predict future outcomes. Common supervised learning algorithms include:

- Linear Regression: Suitable for predicting continuous numeric values.
- Logistic Regression: Applicable for binary classification problems.
- Decision Trees: Effective for both classification and regression tasks.
- Random Forests: A powerful ensemble algorithm that combines multiple decision trees.
- Support Vector Machines: Useful for binary and multi-class classification problems.

2. Unsupervised Learning Algorithms: These algorithms are useful for finding patterns and relationships in data without pre-existing labels. Common unsupervised learning algorithms include:

- K-means Clustering: Used to group similar data points together based on feature similarity.
- Hierarchical Clustering: Suitable for creating tree-like representations of data objects.
- Principal Component Analysis (PCA): Helpful for dimensionality reduction and visualizing high-dimensional data.

3. Reinforcement Learning Algorithms: These algorithms learn through interaction with an environment. They aim to maximize a reward signal by taking optimal actions. Common reinforcement learning algorithms include:

- Q-Learning: Utilized for solving Markov Decision Processes problems.
- Deep Q-Networks (DQN): Combines deep neural networks and reinforcement learning techniques.
- Policy Gradient: Used to train models that generate actions according to a learned policy.

When selecting algorithms, it is crucial to consider the complexity of your problem and the characteristics of your data. Experimenting with multiple algorithms and evaluating their performance using appropriate evaluation metrics will help you determine the most suitable algorithm for your task.

4.2.2 Model Architecture:
Once you have selected an algorithm, designing the right model architecture is essential to enhance the learning capability of your machine learning model. A well-structured model architecture can ensure optimal performance and utilization of computational resources. Let's explore some crucial considerations for designing an effective model architecture:

1. Input and Output Layers: It is crucial to define the correct number of input and output nodes. The input layer should match the dimensionality of your input data, while the output layer should match the desired output format (e.g., binary, multi-class, continuous).

2. Hidden Layers and Neurons: The number of hidden layers and neurons within each layer plays a crucial role in a model's capacity to learn complex patterns. While larger neural networks can capture intricate relationships, they may also lead to overfitting. Experimentation and finding the right balance is key.

3. Activation Functions: Activation functions introduce non-linearities in the model, enabling it to learn complex relationships beyond linear combinations. Common activation functions include sigmoid, tanh, and ReLU (Rectified Linear Unit). Selecting the appropriate activation function will depend on the problem and the requirements of the model.

4. Regularization Techniques: Overfitting is a common concern in machine learning models. Regularization techniques, such as L1 and L2 regularization, dropout, and batch normalization, help combat overfitting and improve generalization.

5. Optimizers: Optimizers determine how the model's weights and biases are updated during the training process. Popular optimizers include stochastic gradient descent (SGD), Adam, and RMSProp. Different optimizers have their unique characteristics, and selecting the right one can significantly influence training speed and convergence.

6. Hyperparameter Tuning: The selection of hyperparameters, such as learning rate, batch size, and epoch count, significantly impacts model training. Applying techniques like grid search, random search, or Bayesian optimization can aid in finding the optimal hyperparameter values.

Understanding the various nuances of designing a model architecture requires hands-on experience and continuous improvement. Experimenting with different architectures, leveraging libraries and frameworks, and staying up to date with the latest research papers and techniques provide valuable insights into creating efficient and effective models.

To summarize, algorithm selection and model architecture play integral roles in the success of machine learning projects. Carefully selecting the appropriate algorithm based on the problem type and data characteristics, combined with well-designed model architectures, can lead to accurate and efficient predictive models. Continuous learning, experimentation, and adaptation are key to mastering algorithm selection and model architecture in the dynamic field of machine learning.

4.3 Data Splitting for Training and Validation

4. 3 Data Splitting for Training and Validation

Machine learning algorithms learn from data. As a beginner in the field of machine learning, it is important to understand the importance of splitting data into training and validation sets. Amidst the pages of this section, we will explore the rationale behind data splitting and the methods to accomplish it effectively.

4. 3. This segregation of data helps us measure how well the model can generalize on unseen or new data. Thus, it is crucial to strike a balance between achieving better accuracy on the training set and ensuring meaningful generalization on new data.

Typically, data splitting involves dividing the available dataset into three subsets: the training set, the validation set, and the test set. The training set is where the model will learn from the patterns and relationships within the data. The validation set assists in adjusting the model's hyperparameters and monitoring its performance during training. Finally, the test set allows us to determine the model's ultimate performance by evaluating it on unseen data.

4. 3. 2 Cross-Validation Technique
One way to achieve a balanced separation of data into training and validation sets is through a technique called cross-validation. Cross-validation is commonly used when the dataset does not have an independent test set available or is too limited in size to allow for a separate test set.

The most prevalent form of cross-validation is "k-fold cross-validation," where the data is divided into k equal-sized folds or partitions. The model is then trained and evaluated k times, each time using a different fold as the validation set, and the remaining k-1 folds combined as the training set. The evaluation results from these k iterations are averaged to obtain an overall performance measure.

The advantage of cross-validation is that all available data is used, ensuring good model generalization. It is particularly beneficial for limited datasets, preventing overfitting that can occur if the model is solely trained on a small portion of the data.

4. 3. 3 Random Data Splitting into Training and Validation Sets
Alternatively, when a separate test set is available, or the dataset is large enough to allow for a relatively large validation set, a simpler approach is to perform a random split of the data. The dataset can be randomly shuffled, and a proportion of the data is allocated for training, validation, and testing. A common split ratio is 70% for training, 15% for validation, and 15% for testing. However, these ratios can vary depending on factors such as the dataset size, complexity, and available resources.

Random splitting works well when individual data samples are similar and there is no particular temporal or spatial ordering to the samples. It is important to ensure that the splitting is done randomly to avoid any bias.

4. 3. 4 Stratified Data Splitting
In certain cases, there might be class imbalance or uneven distribution of samples across different categories or classes in the dataset. To address this issue, stratified data splitting can be employed. Stratified splitting ensures that the class representation in the training, validation, and test sets remains consistent with the overall distribution.

In stratified data splitting, the dataset is divided while maintaining the proportion of samples from each class in each subset. This technique is often used when the models need to be trained on imbalanced datasets or when certain class characteristics are crucial to the overall problem.

4.3.5 The Importance of Data Splitting

Data splitting is crucial in machine learning for several reasons. Firstly, it allows us to measure model performance and determine if it can generalize well on new, unseen data. By evaluating the model on independent validation and test sets, we can estimate its true performance and avoid being overly optimistic based solely on training set accuracy.

Secondly, data splitting helps prevent overfitting, where the model becomes too specialized on the training set and fails to generalize on different instances. The presence of a validation set allows us to tune model hyperparameters to find the optimal configuration that provides good performance while avoiding overfitting.

Finally, data splitting facilitates rigorous experimentation and comparison of different models, algorithms, or architectures. By using consistent data splits, we can make fair performance comparisons under varying circumstances.

4.3.6 Conclusion

In conclusion, data splitting plays a vital role in machine learning. The practice of dividing data into training, validation, and test sets allows us to estimate model performance, prevent overfitting, and conduct fair experiments. Through techniques like cross-validation, random splitting, and stratified splitting, we can ensure optimal generalization and accurate evaluation of machine learning models.

4.4 HandsOn: Building and Training Your First Model

4.4 Hands-On: Building and Training Your First Model

Now that you have a solid understanding of the fundamentals of machine learning, it's time to roll up your sleeves and delve into the exciting world of building and training your first model. Within the context of this hands-on chapter, we will guide you through the step-by-step process, ensuring that you gain practical experience along with theoretical knowledge. So let's get started!

1. Define the problem:
Before diving into model building, you must clearly define the problem you want to solve. This could be predicting house prices, classifying images, sentiment analysis of customer reviews, or any other task you find interesting. Clearly defining your problem is the foundation for developing an effective model.

2. Gather and preprocess data:
The quality of your dataset greatly influences model performance. Collect data that is relevant to your problem and ensure it represents a diverse set of scenarios. Remember to clean and preprocess the data by handling missing values, removing outliers, and scaling or normalizing the features, as necessary.

3. Split the data:
To effectively evaluate your model's performance, you need to split your dataset into training and testing samples. Typically, 80% of the data is allocated for training and the remaining 20% for testing. This ensures that your model generalizes well to

unseen examples. Advanced techniques like cross-validation can be used when you have limited data.

4. Choose an algorithm:
The choice of algorithm depends on the problem at hand, dataset characteristics, and your expertise. Linear regression, decision trees, k-nearest neighbors, support vector machines, or deep learning models like neural networks are some popular choices you can explore. Research and understand the strengths and limitations of each algorithm before selecting the most suitable one.

5. Prepare the algorithm:
Next, it's time to configure and prepare your chosen algorithm. This involves defining the input features, setting hyperparameters (e.g., learning rate, regularization strength), and determining the appropriate measurement of performance (e.g., accuracy, mean squared error). Properly configuring your algorithm greatly impacts the quality of results.

6. Train the model:
Use the training data to instruct your algorithm to learn from the available patterns. During training, adjust the model's internal parameters iteratively to minimize the given loss function. Choose an appropriate optimization algorithm (e.g., stochastic gradient descent) and decide on the number of iterations or epochs. Monitoring the training process enables you to detect overfitting or underfitting and apply necessary remedies.

7. Evaluate the model:
Once your model is trained, use the testing data to evaluate its performance. Compute evaluation metrics (e.g., precision, recall, F1 score, confusion matrix) to understand how well your model is performing. If the model does not meet your expectations, revisit earlier stages to improve its performance. This iterative process is a norm in machine learning, as no model is perfect straight away.

8. Fine-tune and optimize the model:

To enhance your model's performance, you may need to fine-tune and optimize it. Various strategies exist for that purpose, such as feature engineering, hyperparameter tuning, and regularization techniques. Continuously experiment with these approaches until you achieve the desired performance level.

9. Test the model in real-world scenarios:
Testing your model in real-world scenarios is crucial to ensure it performs well beyond the controlled training and testing environments. Gather more data, run it through your model, and measure its performance against real-world ground truth or expert judgment. Learning from how your model performs in production scenarios can guide further improvements.

10. Iterate and improve:
Machine learning is an iterative process. As you learn more about your dataset, problem, and modeling techniques, continue refining and improving your models. Engage in active discussions with the community, learn from open-source projects, and explore advanced topics related to interpretability, fairness, and robustness, which can help you build more sophisticated models.

You have built and trained your first machine learning model. By immersing yourself in the hands-on experience, you have gained invaluable insights into the intricacies of model development. Through experimentation, practice, and persistence, you will continue to enhance your skills and advance beyond this initial milestone. Remember, the road to becoming a proficient machine learning practitioner is an exciting journey that requires continuous learning and application.

Chapter 5: Model Evaluation and Metrics

Model Evaluation and Metrics

1. Training and Test Sets
- The need for dividing data into training and test sets
- Avoiding overfitting by evaluating the model independently on unseen data
- Common techniques for data splitting (e. g. , random sampling, k-fold cross-validation)

3. Common Evaluation Metrics
- Accuracy: measuring the overall correctness of the model's predictions
- Precision, Recall, and F1 Score: balancing between false positives and false negatives
- Confusion Matrix: visual representation of the classification results
- ROC and AUC: assessing the quality of binary classifiers using receiver operating characteristic curves and area under the curve
- Mean Absolute Error and Mean Squared Error: evaluating regression models
- Explain the pros and cons of each metric and when to use them appropriately.

4. Precision-Recall Trade-off
- Understanding the trade-off between precision and recall
- Focusing on specific problem requirements (e. g. , spam detection emphasizes precision, while fraud detection emphasizes recall)
- Choosing appropriate evaluation metrics based on available resources and problem constraints

5. Evaluating Classification Models
- Accuracy as a basic evaluation metric
- Computing precision, recall, and F1 score for classification models
- Interpreting a confusion matrix to understand the model's strengths and weaknesses

6. Evaluating Regression Models
- Mean Absolute Error and Mean Squared Error as metrics for regression models
- Using these metrics to assess the difference between predicted values and actual values
- Applying appropriate scaling techniques to ensure consistency in metric interpretation

7. Considering Business and Problem Context
- Discussing the significance of domain expertise in model evaluation
- Highlighting how different evaluation metrics align with business goals
- Weighing the potential impacts and consequences of false positives and false negatives in specific applications

8. Model Selection Techniques
- Utilizing various model performance measures to compare algorithms
- Cross-validation and averaging to reduce bias in model selection
- Assessing generalization performance for choosing the best model

9. Impact of Imbalanced Datasets
- Addressing the challenges posed by imbalanced datasets in model evaluation
- Techniques to handle class imbalance (e. g. , oversampling, undersampling, and threshold adjustment)
- Evaluating models with imbalanced datasets using appropriate metrics (e. g. , area under the precision-recall curve)

10. Hyperparameter Tuning and Model Evaluation
- The influence of hyperparameters on model performance
- Grid search and randomized search methods for hyperparameter tuning
- Using nested cross-validation for reliable model evaluation during hyperparameter optimization

11. Deploying and Monitoring Models
- Transitioning from model evaluation to deployment in real-world applications
- Establishing monitoring mechanisms for continuously assessing model performance
- Handling model decay and adapting the monitoring process over time

12. Conclusion
- Recap of the importance of model evaluation and metrics
- The evolving nature of model evaluation in response to changing data and problem requirements
- Encouragement to embrace ongoing learning and experimentation for achieving better model evaluations.

5.1 The Importance of Robust Model Evaluation

In the realm of machine learning, model evaluation is a crucial step that determines the performance and effectiveness of our trained models. Accurate and reliable assessment of our models is vital for making informed decisions, solving problems, and achieving successful outcomes. However, model evaluation is not a one-size-fits-all approach since there are various evaluation methods available, and each has its advantages and limitations. Embraced by this section, we will delve into the importance of robust model evaluation and discuss the techniques that novice machine learning practitioners can utilize to evaluate their models effectively.

Robust model evaluation allows us to understand how well our models are performing by quantifying their predictive ability, generalization capability, and their capacity to handle unseen data. It helps us to assess how accurately our models can map input data to the desired outputs and whether they have learned meaningful patterns or simply memorized the training data. Additionally, robust evaluation enables us to compare different models or algorithms, highlighting their relative strengths and weaknesses. This information empowers us to select the most suitable models for our specific tasks and adjust them for optimal performance.

Now, let's explore some essential techniques in robust model evaluation:

1. Train-Test Split:
Often, datasets are divided into two subsets: one for training the model, and the other for testing its performance. This approach, known as train-test split, allows us to evaluate the model on data

it has not seen during training. It provides an estimate of how well the model might perform when facing unseen data. However, this technique has its limitations. For instance, random splits might lead to inefficient models due to the presence of outliers or imbalance in the distribution of classes or labels. Thus, it is crucial to ensure our training set is representative of the entire dataset and avoids any bias.

2. Cross-Validation:
Cross-validation is a more refined approach compared to the train-test split. It overcomes some limitations by partitioning the data into multiple subsets called folds. The model is trained and evaluated on different combinations of these folds, providing a more robust estimation of its performance. One famous technique is k-fold cross-validation, where data is divided into k equally-sized folds, and each fold serves as a testing set while the remaining folds form the training set iteratively. By averaging the results of each fold, we obtain a more reliable evaluation metric. Cross-validation effectively mitigates the impact of random splits and reduces sensitivity to the specific training-testing data division.

3. Performance Metrics:
Evaluating model performance requires suitable metrics that can effectively communicate its predictive accuracy. Common evaluation metrics include accuracy, precision, recall, F1 score, and area under the ROC curve (AUC-ROC). Accuracy measures the overall correctness of predictions, while precision measures the rate of true positives among predicted positives. Recall calculates the rate of true positives among all actual positives. The F1 score combines both precision and recall into a single measure. AUC-ROC provides information about the model's ability to distinguish between classes in binary classification tasks.

4. Overfitting and Underfitting:
Model evaluation also helps us identify whether our models suffer from overfitting or underfitting. Overfitting occurs when the model performs exceptionally well on the training data but

generalizes poorly to unseen data. It usually happens when the model overly complex and captures noise in the training data rather than learning useful patterns. Underfitting, on the other hand, arises when the model fails to capture the underlying patterns in the training data, resulting in low accuracy on both training and testing sets. Evaluating the model performance under different conditions can mitigate these issues, allowing us to strike a balance between underfitting and overfitting.

5. Model Selection:
Robust model evaluation aids in selecting the most suitable model for a particular task. Evaluating several models or algorithms using the same robust evaluation techniques allows us to compare their performance metrics and select the one that best meets our requirements. It's important to evaluate models with different complexities, tune hyperparameters, and investigate their generalization ability across various data samples. This process ensures that we choose the most appropriate algorithm for our problem, leading to improved results and reducing chances of making erroneous predictions.

In conclusion, robust model evaluation is of utmost importance in machine learning. It provides critical insights into the performance and limitations of our models, aiding decision-making and driving progress. Through techniques such as train-test splitting, cross-validation, the selection of appropriate performance metrics, detection of overfitting and underfitting, and model selection, beginners can master the art of evaluating machine learning models effectively. Robust model evaluation enables us to harness the true potential of machine learning and contribute to the advancement of intelligent systems in various fields.

5.2 Common Evaluation Metrics: Accuracy, Precision, Recall

In machine learning, the performance evaluation of a model is essential to assess its effectiveness in solving problems and making predictions. This evaluation process involves the use of various metrics to gauge different aspects of the model's performance. Among these metrics, three commonly used evaluation measures are accuracy, precision, and recall. Amidst the details of this section, we will explore these evaluation metrics in detail, shedding light on their definitions, applications, and how they differ from each other.

5.2.1 Accuracy

Accuracy is perhaps the most intuitive evaluation metric, representing the proportion of correctly predicted instances over the total number of instances. In other words, accuracy measures the ratio of correct predictions to the total number of predictions made by the model. It provides an overall assessment of the correctness of predictions made by the model.

Formally, accuracy is calculated by dividing the number of correct predictions (true positives and true negatives) by the sum of correct and incorrect predictions (true positives, false positives, true negatives, and false negatives).

Accuracy = (True Positives + True Negatives) / (True Positives + False Positives + True Negatives + False Negatives)

While accuracy is informative about the model's performance, it is not suitable for all scenarios. It is particularly problematic in imbalanced classes, where the distribution of classes is uneven. In such cases, even a model that tends to classify most instances into the majority class can achieve high accuracy. Therefore, the reliance on accuracy alone may lead to incorrect conclusions about the effectiveness of the model.

5.2.2 Precision

Precision provides a measure of the accuracy of positive predictions made by the model. It focuses on the ratio of true positives (correct positive predictions) to the sum of true positives and false positives (incorrect positive predictions). Precision serves as a valuable metric in scenarios where avoiding false positives is crucial.

Precision = True Positives / (True Positives + False Positives)

In simpler terms, precision assesses the proportion of correctly predicted positive cases out of all instances that were predicted as positive. Higher precision indicates a lower rate of false positives, implying that the model avoids mistakenly classifying negative instances as positive.

For instance, in a medical diagnosis application, high precision ensures that the model prioritizes accurately identifying true instances of a disease and avoids falsely diagnosing healthy patients.

5.2.3 Recall

Recall, also known as sensitivity or true positive rate, measures the proportion of true positive predictions made by the model compared to all actual positive instances in the dataset. It focuses on the ability of the model to correctly identify positive cases, irrespective of how many false positives it predicts. Recall is particularly useful in scenarios where minimizing false negatives is critical.

Recall = True Positives / (True Positives + False Negatives)

Essentially, recall provides insights into the model's ability to detect all instances of the positive class. A higher recall value implies that the model can identify a larger proportion of actual positive instances accurately.

In a real-world application, such as email filtering, high recall ensures that the model doesn't miss out on classifying spam emails correctly. It would rather categorize some legitimate emails as spam (false positives) than failing to identify actual spam emails (false negatives).

5.2.4 Trade-off Between Precision and Recall

Precision and recall are often inversely related, creating a trade-off between the two metrics. Increasing one generally leads to a decrease in the other.

To optimize these metrics according to the requirements of specific applications, one can adjust the classification threshold of the model. When the classification threshold is decreased, more instances are classified as positive, which increases recall but may decrease precision. Conversely, increasing the threshold results in higher precision but often at the cost of decreased recall.

The balance between precision and recall depends on the specific application and its associated consequences of false positives and false negatives. Therefore, understanding the trade-off between these metrics is crucial in choosing the most suitable evaluation metric for a particular machine learning problem.

5.2.5 Beyond Accuracy, Precision, and Recall

While accuracy, precision, and recall are among the core evaluation metrics in machine learning, they are not the only ones available. Depending on the specific problem at hand, various other metrics such as F1 score, ROC-AUC, and log-loss can also be used.

The F1 score is the harmonic mean of precision and recall,

providing a comprehensive trade-off between the two. It becomes particularly useful in imbalanced datasets, where high accuracy can be misleading.

The Receiver Operating Characteristic (ROC) curve and the Area Under the Curve (AUC) metric provide insights into the model's performance at various classification thresholds. They are beneficial when quantifying the trade-off between true positive rate and false positive rate is necessary.

Lastly, log-loss, or logarithmic loss, is an evaluation metric suitable for probabilistic models. Instead of considering binary decisions, it measures the alignment between predicted probabilities and the true labels. Minimizing log-loss encourages models to produce confident and well-calibrated predictions.

By carefully selecting appropriate evaluation metrics and understanding their implications, you can effectively assess the performance of your machine learning models. These metrics provide valuable insights into your model's strengths and weaknesses and guide you in making data-driven decisions, ensuring the best possible outcomes for your machine learning projects.

5.3 Receiver Operating Characteristic (ROC) Curve

In the world of machine learning, the Receiver Operating Characteristic (ROC) curve is a powerful tool used to evaluate the performance of a classification model. It provides a comprehensive analysis of the trade-off between the true positive rate (TPR) and the false positive rate (FPR) for various threshold values.

Effectively interpreting the ROC curve can be instrumental in understanding the effectiveness of a machine learning model. It allows for a deeper analysis of how well a model can distinguish between different classes and makes critical decisions based on this discrimination.

To begin with, let's understand how the ROC curve is constructed. We start by generating a series of different classification thresholds using the predicted probabilities from our model. These thresholds designate the point at which we will label a predicted outcome as positive or negative.

For every threshold, we calculate the TPR and FPR. TPR, also referred to as sensitivity or recall, measures the proportion of correctly detected positive instances out of all the actual positive instances. Conversely, FPR reflects the ratio of incorrectly classified negative instances out of all the actual negative instances. Together, these two metrics create the groundwork for constructing the ROC curve.

The construction of the ROC curve is straightforward. We plot the FPR on the X-axis and the TPR on the Y-axis for each threshold value. Each point on the ROC curve represents a specific threshold and indicates the corresponding TPR and FPR values. When the ROC curve is closer to the top-left corner, it signifies a higher classification performance. Essentially, the goal is to maximize true positives and minimize false positives, resulting in the curve bending close to the upper left of the graph.

Typically, the area under the ROC curve (AUC-ROC) is used as a quantifiable metric to evaluate the performance of a classification model. A perfect classifier would have an AUC-ROC value of 1, indicating that it perfectly discriminates between classes. On the other hand, a classifier with an AUC-ROC value of 0.5 signifies that it classifies instances no better than random chance.

The AUC-ROC metric allows for easy comparison of different models, as higher values show better classification performance. It overcomes the limitations of metrics like accuracy or error rate, which only provide a binary evaluation of correct or incorrect classification.

Apart from assessing model performance, the ROC curve can also assist in selecting an appropriate threshold value for classification tasks. The choice of threshold significantly impacts the balance between TPR and FPR. By examining the curve and considering specific requirements or tolerances, a threshold can be chosen that aligns with the desired trade-off between the two rates. This facilitates an optimal decision-making process for any given application.

While the ROC curve is an effective tool for evaluating binary classification models, it may not provide a comprehensive analysis for multi-class problems. In these cases, variations, such as the one-vs-all ROC or the micro/macro-averaged ROC curves, can adequately address the challenges posed by multiple classes.

To conclude, the ROC curve presents a comprehensive analysis of classification model performance, capturing the trade-off between true positives and false positives for varying classification thresholds. Its construction showcases the ability of a model to effectively discriminate between different classes, while the AUC-ROC metric quantifies this performance in a single numerical value. By leveraging the insights provided by the ROC curve, data scientists and machine learning practitioners can make informed decisions regarding model development and deployment, leading to enhanced accuracy and performance in real-world applications.

5.4 Interpreting Evaluation Results and Model Selection

After training a machine learning model, evaluating its performance is essential to determine its effectiveness. This process involves interpreting evaluation results and selecting the model that best suits the given problem. Inside this section, we will delve into the nuances of interpreting evaluation metrics and provide guidance on model selection.

5.4.1 Evaluation Metrics

Various evaluation metrics serve different purposes and help us understand the model's performance. Here, we will discuss some commonly used evaluation metrics:

5.4.1.1 Accuracy:
Accuracy is the most straightforward metric, representing the percentage of correct predictions made by the model. While it is widely utilized, accuracy alone might not be an ideal measure for imbalanced datasets as it can yield misleading results. For instance, if we have a dataset with 90% of one class and 10% of the other, a model could achieve 90% accuracy by simply predicting the majority class. Therefore, it is crucial to consider additional evaluation metrics for a comprehensive understanding.

5.4.1.2 Precision, Recall, and F1-Score:
Precision measures the proportion of correctly predicted positive instances out of the total predicted positive instances. Recall, also known as sensitivity, represents the proportion of correctly predicted positive instances out of the actual positive instances in the dataset. F1-score combines precision and recall into a single metric, balancing both measures. Precision is helpful in

scenarios where false positives must be minimized, whereas recall is crucial in situations where missing positive instances can have severe consequences. F1-score provides a harmonic mean between these two metrics, offering a balanced evaluation.

5.4.1.3 Receiver Operating Characteristic (ROC) Curve and Area Under the Curve (AUC):

ROC curves and AUC are widely used in scenarios where the prediction involves probabilities rather than hard classifications. Instead of outputting class labels, some models provide probability scores. The ROC curve provides a visualization of how the model's true positive rate (sensitivity) and false positive rate (1-specificity) change with different probability thresholds. By analyzing the curve's behavior, we can select an appropriate threshold according to our requirements. AUC denotes the area under the ROC curve; a higher value signifies superior model performance.

5.4.1.4 Mean Absolute Error (MAE) and Root Mean Squared Error (RMSE):

For regression problems, evaluation metrics like MAE and RMSE are employed. MAE calculates the average absolute difference between the predicted values and the true values. On the other hand, RMSE measures the standard deviation of these differences, providing more weight to larger errors. These metrics help quantify the model's errors and steer decision-making on model selection or adjustments.

5.4.2 Model Selection

Evaluating multiple models and selecting the most appropriate one for a given task is a vital step in machine learning. Here, we outline the key considerations for model selection.

5.4.2.1 Performance Stability:

A robust model should perform consistently across different datasets or subsets of the same dataset. It is recommended to employ techniques, such as cross-validation, to assess performance stability. Cross-validation involves dividing the dataset into multiple parts and iteratively training and evaluating models on different partitions. By analyzing the models' average performance and standard deviations, we can identify stability and select the model that exhibits the least variance.

5.4.2.2 Bias-Variance Tradeoff:
Models can suffer from either underfitting or overfitting. Underfitting occurs when the model is too simplistic to understand the underlying patterns in the data, resulting in poor performance. Overfitting, on the other hand, happens when the model becomes excessively complex and starts memorizing the training data, failing to generalize well to new, unseen data. Achieving an optimal balance between these extremes can be elusive, but selecting a model with appropriate complexity is crucial. Techniques such as regularization can help mitigate overfitting.

5.4.2.3 Model Complexity and Interpretability:
Different models possess varying levels of complexity. Simpler models, such as linear regression, decision trees, or logistic regression, are easier to understand but might sacrifice predictive performance. On the other hand, complex models like deep neural networks might offer superior predictive capabilities but can be more challenging to interpret. Choosing a model that strikes the right balance between complexity and interpretability is important, especially when the stakeholders require transparency in decision-making.

5.4.2.4 Domain-Specific Considerations:
Domain-specific knowledge plays a vital role in model selection. Factors such as dataset availability, feature interpretation, computational resources required, and industry-specific constraints directly influence the choice of model. It is essential to consult with domain experts to incorporate relevant considerations and domain-specific evaluation metrics into the model selection process.

By examining evaluation metrics and considering key model

selection factors, one can navigate the challenges of interpreting evaluation results and choose an appropriate machine learning model. Remember, a holistic understanding of the performance metrics alongside domain-specific considerations will help you make informed decisions, leading to the development of robust and reliable models.

Chapter 6: Feature Selection and Importance

Feature Selection and Importance
Feature selection is a critical process in machine learning that involves identifying and selecting the most relevant features from a given dataset. By choosing the right features, we can improve the performance, efficiency, and interpretability of our machine learning models. Amidst this chapter, we will delve into the concept of feature selection and importance, understanding various techniques, and their significance in enhancing the overall quality of our models.

1. What is Feature Selection.
1. 1 Definition and Importance
Feature selection refers to the process of selecting a subset of the available features or variables from the dataset used in a machine learning model. It aims to choose the most relevant, informative, and non-redundant features, thereby reducing the complexity and improving the efficiency during model training and predictions.
1. 2 Benefits of Feature Selection
i. Enhanced model performance: By selecting relevant features, we can improve prediction accuracy, model robustness against noise, and generalization.
ii. Reduced model complexity: Feature selection helps in reducing overfitting and avoids the inclusion of irrelevant or redundant features, thus simplifying the models.
iii. Faster computation: Selecting fewer features reduces computational complexity, leading to quicker model training and inference times.
iv. Improved model interpretability: A smaller set of features improves the explainability and interpretability of the learned patterns and relationships present in the data.

2. Feature Importance Techniques:

2.1 Univariate Selection

Univariate selection methods involve analyzing each attribute or feature individually using statistical tests or ranking criteria. Some popular techniques under univariate selection are:

i. Chi-square test for categorical features: This test measures the correlation between categorical features and class labels, determining their level of association or independence.

ii. ANOVA F-test for numerical features: This statistical test analyzes the variation between group means, estimating the significance and impact of features on the target variable.

iii. Information Gain and Gini Index: These measures are widely used in decision tree-based algorithms, identifying the attribute that brings the most information about the target value.

2.2 Wrapper Methods

Wrapper methods build and evaluate several models using different subsets of features, measuring their performance metrics (e.g., accuracy, precision, recall) to select optimal features. Some widely used wrapper methods are:

i. Recursive Feature Elimination (RFE): This technique starts with all features, fits the model, calculates feature importance, and recursively eliminates the least important feature until the desired number of features is achieved.

ii. Genetic algorithms: These evolutionary algorithms mimic the process of natural selection, generating different sets of features and evolving them based on the fitness function, which is typically the model's predictive performance.

2.3 Embedded Methods

Embedded methods are feature selection techniques incorporated within the model training process itself. They evaluate the feature importance as the model is being built, giving rise to a streamlined feature selection approach. Two commonly used embedded methods include:

i. L1 Regularization (LASSO): This method adds an L1 penalty term to the model's objective function, which encourages the coefficients of irrelevant features to reduce to zero during

training.
ii. Tree-based Importance: Decision tree-based algorithms, such as Random Forest and Gradient Boosting, calculate the feature importance based on how much a feature reduces the impurity or error at each node split.

3. Feature Selection Techniques for Different Data Types:
3. 1 Numerical Features
i. Pearson's correlation coefficient: Measures the linear relationship between each pair of numerical features to identify highly correlated or redundant ones.
ii. ANOVA F-test: Determines the significance of a numerical feature concerning multiple classes or groups in the target variable.
iii. Variance thresholding: Eliminates features with low variance, considering them as less informative.

3. 2 Categorical Features
i. Chi-square test: Evaluates the independence between categorical features and the target variable.
ii. Mutual Information: Measures the mutual dependence between categorical variables and the target, providing a good indication of their relevance.

3. 3 Mixed Data Types
For datasets containing a mix of numerical and categorical features, techniques such as Mutual Information with Histogram Binning and Recursive Feature Addition (RFA) can be employed for feature selection.

4. Handling High-Dimensional Data:
Performing feature selection and importance in high-dimensional datasets often presents challenges due to the sheer number of features. To address this, we can employ techniques like:
i. Dimensionality reduction techniques: Methods such as Principal Component Analysis (PCA) and t-SNE can help compress the features into a lower-dimensional space while preserving the most important characteristics.

ii. Feature importance ranking: Ranking features based on their importance and selecting a predefined number of top-ranked features.

iii. Domain expertise: Consulting field experts can provide valuable insights into the most relevant features for the specific problem.

Conclusion:

Feature selection and importance play a crucial role in building effective machine learning models. They help in improving model performance, simplifying complexity, reducing computational overheads, and providing interpretability. By understanding different approaches and techniques, you can identify the optimal set of features for your models, ultimately leading to accurate predictions and informed decision-making.

6.1 Understanding Feature Significance

In the exciting world of machine learning, recognizing the importance and significance of various features in a dataset is a crucial aspect. Features serve as input variables that drive the algorithms to derive meaningful insights and make accurate predictions. Gaining a deeper understanding of feature significance allows us to discern which features have a substantial impact on the outcome and which may be irrelevant or redundant. This knowledge enables us to optimize our machine learning models by selecting the most relevant feature set, improving their performance, and making our predictions more precise.

To comprehend feature significance, we must begin by understanding the fundamentals of feature selection, analysis, and interpretation. Let's delve into these key concepts in more detail:

Feature Selection:

Feature selection is the process of identifying the most relevant features from a vast set of variables that contribute significantly to the outcome. It aims to remove irrelevant, noisy, or strongly correlated features that may negatively impact the model's performance. This approach not only fine-tunes the model but also avoids the curse of dimensionality, where excessive features may lead to overfitting or excessive computational costs. Thus, selecting the right set of features becomes a critical task to achieve optimal results.

Various techniques exist for feature selection, including filter methods, wrapper methods, and embedded methods. Filter methods rely on statistical measures or scoring functions to prioritize features based on their relevance to the outcome.

These measures include correlation coefficients, chi-square statistics, or mutual information. Wrapper methods involve iterative processes, where different subsets of features are evaluated by training and testing the model repeatedly. Finally, embedded methods combine feature selection with the model training process itself, making it an intrinsic part of the algorithm. Examples of embedded methods include decision trees, random forests, and gradient boosting.

Feature Analysis:

After selecting the appropriate subset of features, conducting a comprehensive analysis becomes essential. The analysis allows us to gather deeper insights and understand the relationship between features and the outcome variable. By uncovering correlations, dependencies, and patterns, we can identify how a particular feature affects the overall prediction. This step aids in substantiating the significance of individual features and verifying if they align with our expectations or domain knowledge.

Exploratory data analysis (EDA) techniques, such as data visualization, descriptive statistics, and hypothesis testing, can be employed to conduct feature analysis. Visualization techniques, like scatter plots, histograms, box plots, and heatmaps, help us identify trends, patterns, outliers, and potential relationships between features. Descriptive statistics include computing measures like mean, median, standard deviation, and correlations/co-variances between features. Hypothesis testing allows us to determine if a feature significantly influences the outcome variable by comparing means or applying statistical tests.

Interpreting Feature Significance:

Once the feature analysis is complete, interpreting feature significance paves the way for making informed decisions about their impact on predictions. Different machine learning algorithms may vary in their inherent attribute evaluation and feature importance computation techniques. For instance, linear models, such as linear regression or logistic regression, provide direct coefficients that reflect the relationship between each feature and the outcome. Positive coefficients indicate a positive dependency, whereas negative coefficients signify a negative correlation.

In contrast, complex algorithms like decision trees or ensemble methods possess diverse ways of measuring feature importance. Such methods calculate metrics like feature importance scores, Gini impurity, or information gain. These scores outline the significance of each feature impacting the model's ability to split or classify instances optimally. Additionally, techniques like permutation feature importance or SHAP (SHapley Additive exPlanations) values offer insightful ways to ascertain feature significance.

One of the critical challenges of interpreting feature significance lies in the presence of multicollinearity. Multicollinearity arises when features are highly correlated, obscuring their individual importance. In such cases, employing techniques like Principal Component Analysis (PCA) or Ridge regression to reduce linear dependencies among features aids in disentangling their true significance.

In conclusion, understanding feature significance is integral to effectively harness the power of machine learning models. By employing feature selection, conducting comprehensive analysis, and interpreting the significance of individual features, we enhance our ability to build robust and accurate predictive models. This understanding empowers data scientists, analysts, and enthusiasts to exploit the potential of machine learning in diverse domains and make meaningful decisions based on comprehensive feature analysis.

6.2 Techniques for Feature Selection

In machine learning, feature selection plays a vital role in determining which data attributes or features are most relevant and influential in making accurate predictions. By selecting the right subset of features, we can improve the model's performance, reduce computational overhead, enhance interpretability, and mitigate the risk of overfitting. Housed within this section, we will explore various techniques for feature selection that will help you make informed decisions while developing your machine learning models.

1. Univariate Selection:
Univariate selection is a simplistic yet effective technique to select features based on their individual predictive power. This method involves applying statistical tests to quantify the correlation between each feature and the target variable. Features with the highest statistical scores, such as chi-squared test for categorical variables or correlation coefficients for numerical variables, are chosen as the most informative ones. However, it doesn't consider feature interactions and may overlook valuable relationships involving multiple features.

2. Feature Importance:
Feature importance refers to a family of techniques that determine the relevance of features based on their contribution to a model's overall predictive accuracy. This is typically accomplished by training a machine learning model, such as decision trees, random forests, or gradient boosting, and analyzing the importance or weight assigned to each feature by the model. Features with higher importance scores are considered more influential and are selected for further analysis.

3. Recursive Feature Elimination (RFE):
RFE is an iterative algorithm that starts with all features and

progressively removes the least important ones until a desired number or a pre-specified threshold is reached. The primary idea behind RFE is to measure feature importance by recursively retraining the model using different feature subsets and evaluating their impact on model performance. This technique is particularly useful with models that provide intrinsic feature importance, such as linear regression or support vector machines.

4. L1 regularization (Lasso):
L1 regularization is a technique that involves adding a penalty term proportional to the absolute value of the feature weights to the loss function during model training. This penalty forces less important features to have zero or near-zero weights, effectively performing automatic feature selection. Lasso regularization is especially useful when dealing with high-dimensional data, as it encourages sparsity in the feature space, leaving only the most relevant features for prediction.

5. Tree-based Methods:
Tree-based methods, such as decision trees, random forests, and XGBoost, inherently perform feature selection during their construction process. These algorithms split data based on the most informative features, resulting in readily available measure of feature importance. By utilizing these importance scores, we can select informative features or set appropriate thresholds to prune less critical ones.

6. Regularized Linear Models:
Regularized linear models, such as Lasso and Ridge regression, employ penalty terms to learn valuable features while shrinking or eliminating the less important ones. Ridge regression uses L2 regularization, which reduces the magnitudes of less influential feature weights, but does not eliminate any features. On the other hand, Lasso regression uses L1 regularization to encourage feature selection by driving many feature weights to zero.

7. Correlation Analysis:
Correlation analysis allows us to measure the strength and

direction of the relationship between two variables. By computing correlation coefficients, such as Pearson's correlation for continuous variables or point biserial correlation for categorical variables, we can identify features that have a high correlation with the target variable, indicating their potential predictive value.

8. Forward / Backward Feature Selection:
Forward and backward feature selection are sequential methods that iteratively add or remove features based on their performance during model building. In forward selection, we start with an empty feature set and iteratively add features that provide the most improvement in model performance until desired criteria are met. In backward selection, we initially include all features and progressively remove the least important ones. Both approaches rely on validation metrics, such as accuracy or mean squared error, to decide feature inclusion or exclusion.

These techniques provide a diverse set of tools for feature selection in machine learning. The choice of method largely depends on the dataset characteristics, model type, and desired objectives. Experimentation with different techniques and comparing results will further strengthen your understanding and mastery of feature selection, ultimately leading to more accurate and interpretable machine learning models.

6.3 Handling Categorical and Numerical Features

Machine learning algorithms typically operate on numerical values, yet real-world datasets often include both categorical and numerical features. Therefore, it is crucial to appropriately handle these different types of features to ensure optimal performance and accurate predictions. Entailed within this section, we will delve into various techniques for effectively handling categorical and numerical features in machine learning.

6.3.1 Understanding Categorical Features

Categorical features represent attributes that can be divided into distinct categories or groups. For example, types of cars (Sedan, SUV, Hatchback), education levels (High School, Bachelor's degree, Master's degree), or customer segments (New, Returning, VIP) are types of categorical features.

To handle categorical features, one common approach is to encode them as numerical values. There are multiple encoding methods available, including:

1. Label Encoding: Assigning a unique numerical label to each category. This is useful when categories have some ordinal relationship.

Example: If we have categories [Red, Green, Blue], labeling them as [0, 1, 2] implies an ordinal relation where Blue (2) is greater than Green (1) and Red (0).

2. One-Hot Encoding: Creating new binary features for each category. Each category is condensed into a new binary feature,

and at most, one of these features will have a value of 1 while others would be 0.

Example: If we have categories [Red, Green, Blue], one-hot encoding would convert them into three separate binary features: [1, 0, 0], [0, 1, 0], [0, 0, 1], respectively.

3. Dummy Coding: Similar to one-hot encoding, this method creates binary features for each category, but instead, it includes one less feature than the total number of categories. This approach is useful when a reference category exists for comparison.

Example: For categories [Red, Green, Blue], dummy coding would create only two features: [0, 1] and [0, 0]. Here, [0, 1] represents Green, [0, 0] represents Blue, and Red is the reference category.

4. Target Encoding: Assigning a numerical value to each category based on the mean target value of the corresponding category. This method can capture statistical relationships between features and target distribution.

Example: For a binary classification task with categories [Unfavorable, Favorable]. Target encoding might assign them values based on the corresponding probability (e.g., Unfavorable: 0.2, Favorable: 0.8).

6.3.2 Handling Numerical Features

Numerical features represent continuous or discrete numeric values. Depending on the distribution of these values, specific approaches should be applied to ensure suitable processing.

Some techniques to handle numerical features include:

1. Scaling: Rescaling feature values by transforming them into a common scale. This is particularly useful when working with numerical features that have different units or divergent ranges.

Examples of scaling techniques are Min-Max scaling, where values are scaled between 0 and 1, and Standardization, which scales values based on their mean and standard deviation.

2. Binning: Discretizing continuous numerical features by dividing them into a fixed number of intervals or bins. After binning, numerical features can be treated as categorical variables.

Binning helps in capturing non-linear relationships or addressing outliers. Common binning techniques include Equal-Width and Equal-Frequency binning.

3. Power Transformations: Applying mathematical functions like logarithmic or exponential transformations to rescale skewed distributions. Power transformations can help capture complex relationships that are not easily handled by linear models.

Examples include Box-Cox and Yeo-Johnson transformations, which aim to make the transformed variable follow a Gaussian-like distribution.

4. Interaction Terms: Creating new features by considering interaction between numerical features. This involves mathematical operations such as multiplication or addition.

Interaction terms allow models to capture relationships that can't be effectively expressed with individual features alone. Polynomial features and notations like $x_1 * x_2$ are commonly implemented for this purpose.

5. Handling Missing Values: Dealing with missing numerical values is essential to avoid biased or compromised model predictions. Strategies for handling missing values include imputation approaches such as mean imputation or median imputation.

Additionally, domain-specific knowledge and advanced

imputation techniques like k-nearest neighbors or regression imputation can be employed to handle missing values effectively.

6.3.3 Feature Engineering for Categorical and Numeric Data

In addition to the above techniques, feature engineering plays a crucial role in improving the predictive power of machine learning models. It involves creating new informative features from pre-existing ones.

Transforming or combining both categorical and numerical features can lead to more powerful representations, enhancing model performance. Techniques such as Polynomial Encoding and Bin Counting can be used effectively for feature engineering involving both types of features.

In summary, handling categorical and numerical features in machine learning requires applying various techniques, including encoding, scaling, binning, power transformations, handling missing values, and feature engineering. By thoughtfully processing these features, you can ensure improved accuracy, efficiency, and robustness of machine learning models.

6.4 Best Practices in Feature Engineering

Feature engineering is a crucial step in the machine learning workflow and can significantly impact the performance of a model. It involves selecting, transforming, and creating meaningful features from the raw data, allowing the algorithm to extract relevant patterns and make accurate predictions. Embraced by this section, we will discuss some best practices in feature engineering that can improve the overall performance of your machine learning models.

1. Understand the Domain:
Before jumping into feature engineering, it is imperative to have a solid understanding of the domain you are working in. This knowledge will help you identify which features are likely to be important. Understanding the underlying processes and business requirements can guide you in selecting relevant features that have a strong correlation with the target variable.

2. Feature Selection:
Feature selection involves identifying the most relevant features from a large pool of available variables. It helps in reducing model complexity and enhances interpretability. There are several methods to perform feature selection, such as univariate feature selection, recursive feature elimination, and L1 regularization. Experiment with different techniques and keep evaluating the performance of your model to find the optimal set of features.

3. Handling Missing Data:
Missing data is a common problem in real-world datasets. Ignoring it can lead to biased or unreliable results. Instead, adopt suitable techniques for handling missing data. One

approach is to delete instances or features that contain missing values if you have sufficient data. Another approach is imputation, where missing values are replaced either by a constant value, mean, median, or by modeling the missing variables using other related features. Choose the imputation method based on the characteristics of the dataset and carefully handle missing data to avoid introducing biases into the model.

4. Dealing with Categorical Variables:
Categorical variables are common in many datasets and often provide valuable information. However, most machine learning algorithms work with numerical inputs. One way to handle categorical variables is to perform one-hot encoding. This technique creates binary columns for each category, representing whether the entry falls into that category or not. Another approach is to apply label encoding, which assigns a unique numerical label to each category. However, be cautious with label encoding as it can introduce an arbitrary ranking among the categories. Choose the appropriate technique based on the number of categories and the nature of the variable.

5. Scaling and Normalization:
The scale of different features may vary significantly, which can impact the performance of certain machine learning algorithms. Therefore, it is often crucial to scale or normalize the features to a similar range. Standardization, where each feature is transformed to have zero mean and unit variance, is a common technique used for data scaling. Normalization, also known as min-max scaling, scales the features to a predefined range, typically between 0 and 1. Select the appropriate method based on the requirements of your model and the distribution of the data.

6. Feature Construction:
Feature construction involves generating new features based on a combination of existing ones. This process often requires domain knowledge and creativity. It enables the algorithm to capture complex relationships that might not be apparent in the original dataset. Feature construction could involve arithmetic

operations, such as addition, multiplication, or division, or more complex transformations like interaction terms, polynomial features, or interactions with time. Experiment with different feature construction techniques and evaluate their impact on the model's performance.

7. Regularization and Dimensionality Reduction:
When working with high-dimensional datasets, dimensionality reduction techniques become necessary to simplify feature representation and improve model efficiency. Techniques like principal component analysis (PCA) or linear discriminant analysis (LDA) can help identify important latent variables or projections that represent most of the original data's variance. Regularization techniques, such as L1 or L2 regularization, encourage sparsity in the feature space, keeping only the most relevant features and reducing overfitting.

8. Continuous Monitoring and Iteration:
Feature engineering is an iterative process. It is crucial to continuously monitor your model's performance, validate the impact of the engineered features, and reassess them as you discover new insights in the domain or acquire more data. Regularly evaluate your feature engineering choices to ensure they continue to align with the problem at hand and strive for continuous improvement.

In conclusion, effective feature engineering can significantly enhance the performance of machine learning models. By understanding the domain, selecting relevant features, handling missing data, dealing with categorical variables, scaling or normalizing features, constructing new features, and applying dimensionality reduction techniques, you can improve model accuracy, interpretability, and robustness. Remember that feature engineering is both an art and a science, requiring creativity and a deep understanding of the problem space. As you gain experience, experiment with different techniques to uncover patterns hidden in the data and continuously refine your feature engineering process.

Chapter 7: Neural Networks and Deep Learning

Neural Networks and Deep Learning

Inside this chapter, we will delve into the fascinating world of neural networks and deep learning. Neural networks are a machine learning technique inspired by the functioning of the human brain. Deep learning, on the other hand, refers to the utilization of neural networks with multiple layers. These techniques have proven to be powerful tools for a wide range of applications such as image recognition, natural language processing, and speech recognition. Inside this chapter, we will explore the fundamental components of neural networks, how they work, and the main concepts behind deep learning.

Section 1: The Building Blocks of Neural Networks

1. 1 Neurons and Activation Functions:

To understand neural networks, we need to start with the basic building block: neurons. Neurons mimic the behavior of their biological counterparts and process incoming information using activation functions. This section will explain the role of activation functions in neural networks and shed light on popular types like sigmoid, ReLU, and tanh.

1. 2 Artificial Neural Networks (ANN):

Artificial neural networks consist of multiple connected layers of neurons. Each neuron in one layer is connected to every neuron in the following layer, allowing for efficient information processing. We will discuss the structure of ANNs and how weights and biases are crucial for modeling complex relationships within the data.

1.3 Feedforward and Backpropagation:

The feedforward process in neural networks involves passing the input through each layer, performing weighted calculations, and finally producing an output. The backpropagation algorithm is then used to adjust the weights and biases based on the error generated during the forwarding process. We will delve into the mathematics behind these processes and discuss the importance of gradient descent in optimizing the neural network.

Section 2: Deep Learning and Convolutional Neural Networks (CNN)

2. We will explore the motivation behind deep learning, its advantages, and situations where it outperforms traditional machine learning algorithms.

2.2 Convolutional Neural Networks:

Convolutional Neural Networks (CNNs) are a specific type of deep learning architecture widely employed in computer vision tasks such as image classification and object detection. This section will cover the unique structure of CNNs, including convolutional and pooling layers, and explain how they enable the network to extract meaningful features from images.

2.3 Training CNNs and Transfer Learning:

Training deep networks, particularly CNNs, can be a computationally intensive task. We will discuss techniques to speed up training, such as using modern hardware like GPUs and leveraging pre-trained models through transfer learning.

Section 3: Recurrent Neural Networks (RNN) and Long Short-Term Memory (LSTM)

3.1 Recurrent Neural Networks:

While feedforward neural networks are suitable for processing individual data points, recurrent neural networks (RNNs) are designed to handle sequential data. RNNs maintain memory by allowing connections between neurons to form cycles, enabling them to analyze sequences. We will examine the structure of RNNs and discuss their applications in tasks like speech recognition and translation.

3. 2 Long Short-Term Memory (LSTM):

LSTM is a variant of RNNs designed to overcome the limitations of regular RNNs regarding capturing long-term dependencies. LSTMs introduce memory cells and gating mechanisms that regulate the flow of information, exponentially enhancing the performance of sequential tasks. We will explore the workings of LSTM networks and their role in various applications, such as sentiment analysis and language modeling.

Conclusion:
Neural networks and deep learning have revolutionized the field of machine learning. Inside this chapter, we covered the fundamental components of neural networks, including neurons, activation functions, and feedforward-backpropagation. We then dived into deep learning, specifically CNNs well-suited for computer vision, and RNNs useful for analyzing sequential data. Understanding these concepts will empower you to build and train powerful models that can solve complex real-world problems in image recognition, natural language processing, and much more.

7.1 Introduction to Neural Networks

7. Whether you are a student, a professional, or simply curious about the field of machine learning, understanding neural networks is essential.

Neural networks, also known as artificial neural networks (ANN) or simply "neurons," are computational systems inspired by the interconnected nature of neurons in the human brain. At its core, a neural network consists of an intricate network of artificial neurons, also called nodes or units, that work collaboratively to process and analyze complex patterns or inputs.

The basic building blocks of a neural network are the neurons themselves. Each neuron receives input data, processes it through an activation function, and generates an output. These outputs are then passed to other neurons, forming a network-like structure. The strength or weight assigned to the connections between neurons determines the influence of one neuron's output on another's input.

The structure of a neural network can range from simple to highly complex, depending on the problem being solved. The basic architecture is comprised of various layers, including an input layer, one or more hidden layers, and an output layer. The input layer receives input data, the hidden layers process this data through numerous computations, and the output layer generates the desired result.

What differentiates neural networks from traditional algorithms is their ability to automatically learn and adapt from the input data. This learning is achieved through a process called training, where the neural network is exposed to a set of labeled examples and adjusts its weights and biases to minimize prediction errors.

Over time, the network becomes adept at recognizing patterns and making accurate predictions even when faced with unseen data.

Neural networks have various activation functions that enable them to generate non-linear and complex outputs. Some commonly used activation functions include the sigmoid function, hyperbolic tangent function, and rectified linear unit (ReLU) function. Each activation function exhibits unique characteristics, affecting the network's ability to learn, converge, and generalize.

One of the most popular algorithms used to train neural networks is backpropagation. Backpropagation involves propagating the error in the network's predicted output through the network, adjusting the weights and biases of each neuron layer by layer. Through this iterative process, the network fine-tunes its parameters, improving the accuracy of its predictions.

Neural networks find application in a myriad of fields, from computer vision to natural language processing. They are used in image recognition systems, speech recognition, sentiment analysis, autonomous vehicles, and even medical diagnoses. Their ability to learn complex patterns and generate accurate predictions has revolutionized numerous domains, making them an indispensable tool in today's technological landscape.

In summary, neural networks offer a powerful framework for solving intricate problems in machine learning. By emulating the connections and computations of the human brain, these networks can learn from data, adapt their behavior, and provide accurate predictions. Their architecture, which consists of interconnected layers and neural units, enables them to tackle complex tasks. In the following chapters, we will delve deeper into the inner workings of neural networks and explore specific types of architectures and algorithms that have demonstrated exceptional performance in various domains.

7.2 Core Components: Layers, Neurons, and Weights

Amidst this section, we will delve into the core components of neural networks - layers, neurons, and weights. These fundamental elements play a crucial role in the functioning of machine learning models and understanding them is essential for any beginner stepping into the world of artificial intelligence.

7.2.1 Layers:
Layers are organized sets of neurons that help process and transform inputs to produce desired outputs in a neural network. They form the building blocks of any machine learning model. Each layer consists of a specified number of neurons and brings a specific level of abstraction to the overall computation of the network.

There are typically three types of layers found in most neural networks: input layers, hidden layers, and output layers. The input layer receives raw data as input, while the output layer produces the final prediction or output of the model. The hidden layers, as the name suggests, remain hidden during the training and are responsible for extracting and transforming features from the input data.

Furthermore, these layers can be densely connected, also known as fully connected or dense layers, where each neuron in a specific layer is connected to every neuron in the previous and subsequent layers. On the other hand, there are also specialized layer types like convolutional layers, recurrent layers, and pooling layers, each designed to tackle certain types of data and tasks effectively.

7.2.2 Neurons:

Neurons, often referred to as nodes or perceptrons, are the basic building blocks of neural networks. Inspired by the structure and functioning of neurons in the human brain, neural network neurons receive inputs, process them, and produce outputs that serve as inputs for subsequent layers or form the final prediction of the model.

The core computational unit of a neuron is a nonlinear function that takes a linear combination of its inputs, also called activations, and applies an element-wise activation function. This function introduces nonlinearity to the network, allowing it to learn complex and nonlinear relationships present in the data. Activation functions commonly include sigmoid, tanh, ReLU (Rectified Linear Units), and softmax.

Each neuron is connected to neurons in the previous and subsequent layers through weights. These weights are responsible for capturing the importance or relevance of a particular input and are updated during the training process to optimize the performance of the model.

7.2.3 Weights:

Weights form a crucial part of neural networks as they determine the strength of connections between neurons. They essentially model the influence of each input in the overall computation carried out by the network. Weights are initially assigned random values and iteratively adjusted during the training phase to minimize the model's prediction error.

During the training process, the neural network aims to learn optimal weights that minimize the difference between the predicted output and the true output (the desired target). This optimization is achieved through various techniques such as backpropagation and gradient descent, with the goal of optimizing a predefined loss function.

The process of updating weights involves calculating the gradient of the loss function with respect to each weight and adjusting the weights accordingly to minimize the error. Iterating through multiple training samples, this iterative process helps the neural network "learn" by fine-tuning the weights to find the best possible representation of the underlying patterns in the data.

In a nutshell, layers, neurons, and weights are the bedrock of neural networks. Layers organize neurons, which in turn process inputs and output useful information towards the final prediction or output. Weights provide the necessary flexibility for the network to capture the essence of the data by adjusting their values iteratively through training. By understanding and manipulating these core components, you will acquire a solid foundation in the field of machine learning and be better equipped to build and train neural networks effectively.

7.3 Activation Functions and Backpropagation

In the exciting world of machine learning, one of the fundamental concepts you need to wrap your head around is activation functions and their role in the backpropagation algorithm. Activation functions play a crucial role in determining the output of a neural network and are essential for achieving accurate and reliable predictions. Surrounded by this section, we will delve into the intricacies of activation functions and how they enable the backpropagation algorithm to optimize the network's weights and biases. So fasten your seatbelts and get ready for an in-depth exploration of activation functions and backpropagation!

To comprehend the significance of activation functions, let's start by understanding their role in neural networks. Neural networks consist of interconnected layers of nodes called neurons, and each neuron applies an activation function to the weighted sum of inputs it receives. Activation functions serve as non-linear transformation functions that introduce non-linearity into the network, enabling it to learn complex patterns and relationships in the data.

1. Activation Functions:
Activation functions impose a non-linear element to the output of a neuron and generate the final output of the network. There are various activation functions available, each suitable for different scenarios and network architectures. The most commonly used activation functions include the sigmoid function, the hyperbolic tangent function, and the rectified linear unit (ReLU) function.

a) Sigmoid Function:

The sigmoid function squashes the input values to a range between 0 and 1, making it useful for binary classification problems. However, the gradient of the sigmoid function becomes increasingly small away from the center, leading to the vanishing gradient problem.

b) Hyperbolic Tangent Function:
Similar to the sigmoid function, the hyperbolic tangent function squashes the input values, but this time to the range between -1 and 1. It improves upon the sigmoid function by having a steeper gradient around the origin, but it still suffers from the vanishing gradient problem as the absolute input values increase.

c) Rectified Linear Unit (ReLU) Function:
The ReLU function avoids the vanishing gradient problem encountered by the previously mentioned activation functions by producing a value of zero when the input is negative. For positive inputs, it outputs the input value directly, making it computationally efficient and effective in deep neural networks.

2. Backpropagation:
After understanding the role of activation functions, it's time to explore how they are utilized in the backpropagation algorithm, which is the heart of neural network training. Backpropagation involves updating the network's weights and biases by propagating the error back through the layers of the network. The derivatives or gradients of the activation functions play an important role in this process.

During the forward pass of training, the activation function computes the output of each neuron, which is then fed forward to the subsequent layers. In the backward pass, the gradients of the activation functions are calculated, along with other factors like the error and the network's weights.

The gradients obtained from the activation functions enable the backpropagation algorithm to iteratively adjust the network's weights and biases using optimization methods like stochastic gradient descent (SGD) or Adam. The gradients provide crucial information on how much each weight and bias contributed to the total error of the network, allowing for fine-tuning in subsequent iterations.

3. Choosing Activation Functions:
Selecting an appropriate activation function requires an understanding of the problem at hand and the behavior of different functions. In general, it is advised to start with the ReLU function due to its simplicity and effectiveness. However, if vanishing gradients are anticipated or if the outputs need to be squashed to a specific range, sigmoid or hyperbolic tangent functions can be more suitable.

It's also essential to consider recent advancements in activation functions, such as the Leaky ReLU, which addresses the issue of dead neurons in the ReLU function, or the softmax function, used in multi-class classification tasks. Additionally, techniques like parametric activation functions and adaptive functions hold promise for discovering more efficient activation functions based on the data.

In conclusion, activation functions and backpropagation are fundamental components in training neural networks. The choice of activation function determines the capability of the network to capture complex patterns, while backpropagation optimizes the network's weights and biases. Remember to experiment with different activation functions, keeping in mind the characteristics of your data and the desired output, and witness the impressive power of activation functions in bringing machine learning models to life!

Keep learning and experimenting, and may your understanding of activation functions and backpropagation continue to deepen as you explore the exciting world of machine learning!

7.4 Basic Architectures: Feedforward and Recurrent Networks

In the exciting world of machine learning, there exist two fundamental types of neural network architectures that stand out as the building blocks for many advanced models: Feedforward Networks and Recurrent Networks. Understanding the principles and applications of these architectures is essential for beginners delving into the field of machine learning. Amidst the information in this section, we will explore these two core concepts in detail, highlighting their characteristics, functionalities, and use cases.

7.4.1 Feedforward Networks

Feedforward Networks, also known as feedforward neural networks or multi-layer perceptrons (MLPs), are the most basic and widely used form of artificial neural networks. As the name suggests, the information in these networks travels in a single direction: from the input layer to the output layer, without any feedback connections. This unidirectional flow allows feedforward networks to make predictions or classifications based solely on the given input.

The core architecture of a feedforward network comprises an input layer, one or more hidden layers, and an output layer. Each layer consists of multiple computational units called neurons or nodes, which process and transform the incoming data. These nodes are interconnected through edges, which carry weighted connections that determine the strength of the signals between them. Additionally, every node is associated with an activation function, which introduces non-linearity into the network's computation.

Training a feedforward network involves adjusting the weights of its connections and tuning the activation functions by passing the input data through the network repetitively. This process, known as backpropagation, uses optimization techniques to gradually update the network parameters, minimizing the difference between predicted and actual outputs.

Feedforward networks find applications in a wide range of tasks, such as image and speech recognition, natural language processing, and regression problems. With their ability to model complex patterns and relationships in data, they form the foundation for various advanced architectures that build upon their principles.

7.4.2 Recurrent Networks

Contrasting feedforward networks, Recurrent Networks incorporate feedback connections, allowing the neural network to process not only the current input but also information from previous states or iterations. This temporal persistence in RNNs enables them to model sequential data effectively.

Instead of the simple unidirectional flow in feedforward networks, the information in a recurrent network loops back to the network's earlier stages. Each neuron in a recurrent network maintains a hidden state, which captures the underlying context of the previously seen inputs. This hidden state helps the network to remember long-term dependencies and make informed predictions based on the given sequence of inputs.

Recurrent Networks are well-suited for handling time-series data, language processing tasks such as text generation, speech recognition, sentiment analysis, and many other sequential processes. Long Short-Term Memory (LSTM) networks and Gated Recurrent Units (GRUs) are popular variations of recurrent architectures that have improved capability in handling longer and more complex time dependencies.

While recurrent networks provide excellent performance on

sequential tasks, they often suffer from the "vanishing gradient" problem during training. This issue limits their ability to capture and learn from long sequences, as the gradients propagated backward through time tend to diminish exponentially.

In recent years, newer recurrent architectures and techniques such as Bidirectional Recurrent Networks, Attention Mechanisms, and Transformer models have emerged, overcoming some of these limitations and achieving state-of-the-art results in natural language processing and other related domains. These advancements have made recurrent architectures more versatile and powerful than ever before.

7.4.3 Choosing the Right Architecture

Understanding the characteristics and strengths of feedforward and recurrent networks allows beginners to make informed decisions when selecting an appropriate architecture for their specific application. Generally, feedforward networks excel in tasks where there is no temporal dependency or sequence-related interaction between the data points. On the other hand, recurrent networks shine when the information context and sequential correlations play a crucial role.

Careful consideration should be given to several factors like the nature of the dataset, the expected input-output relationship, and the desired functionality to decide which architecture is best suited for a given problem. Moreover, it is important to consider the inherent limitations of each architecture and explore advanced variants and techniques that have been proposed to overcome these limitations.

In conclusion, feedforward and recurrent networks serve as the foundation for many sophisticated machine learning models. Understanding their architecture, characteristics, and key applications equips beginners with valuable knowledge to venture into the realm of machine learning confidently. Whether it's the straightforward unidirectional flow of feedforward networks or the complex temporal dependencies captured by recurrent networks, each architecture has its domain and plays a vital role in building intelligent systems that can learn from complex data sources.

Chapter 8: Deep Learning Applications

Deep Learning Applications

Amidst the information in this chapter, we will explore the exciting world of deep learning applications. Deep learning, a subset of machine learning, has gained tremendous popularity for its ability to provide breakthrough solutions in various domains. From computer vision, natural language processing, to speech recognition, deep learning models have revolutionized the way we interact with technology. Amidst the information in this chapter, we will delve into some of the most impactful and intriguing applications of deep learning.

8.1 Computer Vision

Deep learning has significantly advanced computer vision by enabling machines to automatically identify and understand visual data. Computer vision applications powered by deep learning algorithms are extensively used in self-driving cars, facial recognition systems, object detection and tracking, medical image analysis, video surveillance, and much more.

Object Detection and Classification: Deep learning models like Convolutional Neural Networks (CNNs) have made significant progress in object recognition and localization. These models can accurately identify and classify objects in images or videos. Applications include self-driving car technologies, where CNNs enable cars to detect and understand traffic signs, pedestrians, and other vehicles on the road.

Facial Recognition: Facial recognition systems powered by deep learning models are capable of identifying individuals in images or videos. These systems have revolutionized security and surveillance applications, unlocking possibilities like hands-free device access, efficient authentication systems, and personalized marketing.

Medical Image Analysis: Deep learning algorithms have demonstrated remarkable success in medical image analysis. Radiologists can leverage deep learning models to detect anomalies in X-ray images, accurately diagnose diseases, and analyze medical scan reports. This technology has the potential to save lives by improving the accuracy and speed of diagnosing critical conditions.

8.2 Natural Language Processing

Another prominent field where deep learning has made a profound impact is natural language processing (NLP). NLP focuses on enabling computers to process, understand, and generate human language. Deep learning models applied to NLP have surpassed many traditional methods and brought advancements in machine translation, sentiment analysis, chatbots, and language generation.

Machine Translation: Deep learning models, specifically recurrent neural networks (RNNs) and transformer models, have significantly enhanced machine translation systems. Technologies like Google Translate capitalize on deep learning techniques to provide accurate translation services for various languages, enabling effective communication across global borders.

Sentiment Analysis: Thanks to deep learning, sentiment analysis has become more accurate and efficient. Sentiment analysis models can analyze large volumes of textual data, such as social media posts and reviews, to gauge people's sentiments towards products, services, or events. Businesses can utilize this information to make data-driven decisions and tailor their strategies accordingly.

Chatbots and Virtual Assistants: Virtual assistants like Apple's Siri, Amazon's Alexa, and Google Assistant are all powered by deep learning models. These models understand natural language queries and provide intelligent responses by using sophisticated algorithms that recognize patterns and context. Chatbots, found in various industries, also leverage deep learning to engage with customers and provide automated assistance.

8.3 Speech Recognition

Deep learning has transformed speech recognition technologies, facilitating broader adoption and driving better accuracy in voice-controlled systems. Speech recognition applications have widespread usage, including voice assistants, transcription services, automated phone services, and language learning applications.

Voice Assistants: The remarkable success of deep learning in speech recognition is evident in voice assistants like Apple's Siri, Amazon's Alexa, and Google Assistant. These assistants understand and respond to voice commands, helping users perform various tasks, such as setting reminders, playing music, or searching the internet.

Transcription Services: Deep learning models have revolutionized the transcription industry. Transcription services can now accurately convert spoken language into written text, saving time and empowering seamless access to information in various sectors, including academia, journalism, and business.

Automated Phone Services: Deep learning-powered speech recognition enables automated phone services to understand customer requests or queries. This technology improves customer service and reduces the wait time, leading to enhanced customer satisfaction.

Language Learning Applications: Innovative language learning apps, utilizing deep learning, have transformed the way we learn foreign languages. These apps leverage speech recognition to analyze learners' pronunciation, provide real-time feedback, and personalize learning experiences.

Amidst the information in this chapter, we have explored just a few of the many significant and fascinating applications of deep learning. The power and potential of deep learning models are vast and continually evolving, opening doors to immense possibilities in numerous domains. As you continue your journey in machine learning, remember to harness the power of deep learning to develop intelligent systems capable of understanding, recognizing, and interacting with the world around us.

8.1 Distinguishing Deep Learning from Traditional ML

Distinguishing Deep Learning from Traditional ML

When delving into the realm of machine learning (ML), it becomes essential to understand the key differences between traditional ML and its more advanced counterpart, deep learning. While both are branches under the broader umbrella of artificial intelligence (AI), they differ significantly in their approaches, architectures, and applications. Amidst the information in this chapter, we will explore these distinctions in depth, providing you with a solid basis for comprehending the intricate world of deep learning.

To comprehend the fundamental differences, it's important to grasp the basic working principles of traditional ML. Traditional ML approaches primarily rely on feature engineering, where domain experts manually extract and select relevant features from raw data before feeding it into learning algorithms for prediction or classification. This feature engineering aspect demands substantial amounts of human effort and expertise. However, it has proven effective for solving various problems such as sentiment analysis, spam detection, or credit scoring.

Deep learning, on the other hand, breaks away from dependence on feature engineering and instead focuses on automating the process of feature extraction. Deep learning techniques learn feature hierarchies directly from raw input data by employing complex neural network architectures. These architectures, typically comprised of multiple layers of interconnected units called neurons, closely approximate the structure and functioning of the human brain. This enables deep learning models to process and understand vast amounts of intricate information with remarkable accuracy and efficiency.

One of the key advantages deep learning offers over traditional ML is its ability to handle unstructured data such as images, audio, and text. While traditional ML techniques struggle to analyze unprocessed raw data directly, deep learning thrives in this domain. By leveraging convolutional neural networks (CNNs) and recurrent neural networks (RNNs), deep learning models excel in image recognition, speech synthesis, natural language processing, and other data-heavy tasks. In essence, deep learning allows machines to learn and replicate the highly intricate processes of human perception and cognition.

Another critical distinction is in the domain of dataset size and training requirements. Traditional ML necessitates a significant amount of domain-specific labeled data for effective training. Limited volumes of data often hinder the performance of traditional ML algorithms. On the contrary, deep learning models thrive on vast datasets, exhibiting enhanced performance as they ingest more information. This reliance on extensive amounts of training data, combined with their ability to scale, makes deep learning exceptionally effective at addressing large-scale problems such as object recognition in images or translating entire documents.

However, deep learning, despite its tremendous potential, exposes its users to several challenges and caveats. Traditional ML models can typically provide interpretable results, allowing domain experts to comprehend the factors contributing to a specific prediction. In contrast, deep learning models often seem black-box-like due to their complex architectures. Although recent efforts have emerged to develop methods for interpreting deep learning models, they remain an ongoing area of research and development.

Additionally, the computational demands of deep learning can be substantial. The network architectures within deep learning models comprise millions (or even billions) of global parameters that require powerful computational resources for training and inference. As deep learning models grow deeper and wider to tackle more complex problems, the hardware and infrastructure demands also increase accordingly. This makes deep learning less accessible to those without significant computational resources.

Finally, ethical considerations arise within the context of deep learning due to its data-hungry nature. In certain scenarios, gathering sufficient domain-specific data might be difficult, costly, or unethical. Consequently, employing deep learning models in contexts without adequate standardization and control can impair the fairness, accountability, and transparency of decision-making systems based on these models.

In summary, the key differentiators between deep learning and traditional ML reside in the automated feature extraction capabilities, handling of unstructured data, reliance on extensive datasets, and the challenges posed by interpretability, computational demands, and ethical aspects. As you embark on your journey to understand machine learning, having a clear distinction between these two branches will significantly enrich your understanding of the vast potential and limitations offered by each. Remember, this is just the beginning of your learning experience—prepare to immerse yourself in the fascinating world of deep learning and traditional ML as you progress in this comprehensive guide.

8.2 Convolutional Neural Networks (CNNs) for Image Tasks

8. 2 Convolutional Neural Networks (CNNs) for Image Tasks

Convolutional Neural Networks (CNNs) have revolutionized the field of computer vision and are widely used for image-related tasks. Captured within this section, we will delve into the basics of CNNs, their architecture, and how they are applied to various image tasks. Prepare to explore the exciting world of Convolutional Neural Networks as we embark on this detailed journey.

8. 2. Neural networks are computational models inspired by the neural structure of the human brain. They consist of interconnected layers of artificial neurons that process and transmit information.

Convolutional Neural Networks, a specific type of neural network architecture, have gained tremendous popularity for their ability to analyze and understand images. They have a unique feature called convolution layers, which are responsible for extracting key features from input images.

8. 2. 2 Understanding the CNN Architecture

CNNs have a sophisticated architecture designed explicitly for image processing tasks. Let's explore the key components of CNNs in detail:

8. 2. 2. 1 Convolutional Layers

Convolutional layers are the heart of CNNs. They apply a convolution operation on the input image, convolving it with a set of learnable filters. These filters scan the image for specific patterns and extract relevant features, such as edges, textures, or shapes.

8.2.2.2 Pooling Layers

Pooling layers follow convolutional layers and reduce the spatial dimensions of the features map, decreasing the computational workload for subsequent layers. Max pooling is a commonly used pooling technique that retains the most relevant information within specific regions.

8.2.2.3 Fully Connected Layers

After several convolutional and pooling layers, fully connected layers are added to simulate the decision-making process. These layers connect every neuron from the previous layer to the next, empowering the network to output final predictions.

8.2.3 Training a CNN

To utilize the power of CNNs, training them with a vast amount of labeled data is crucial. The process involves passing the training images through the network, comparing the predicted outputs with the ground truth labels, and adjusting the network's parameters to minimize the error.

8.2.4 CNNs for Image Classification

Image classification, the task of assigning predefined categories to input images, has been revolutionized by CNNs. CNNs' ability to learn meaningful hierarchical representations of images has significantly boosted classification accuracies, outperforming traditional computer vision techniques.

8.2.5 CNNs for Object Detection

Object detection involves identifying and localizing multiple objects within an image. CNNs have been at the forefront of object detection research due to their remarkable feature extraction capabilities. By combining object proposals and convolutional feature maps, CNNs can robustly detect objects in varying image contexts.

8. 2. 6 CNNs for Image Segmentation

Image segmentation goes a step further than object detection by segregating images into semantically meaningful regions. CNNs, with their ability to capture intricate image features during the training process, have significantly advanced image segmentation. By predicting pixel-level labels, CNNs enable fine-grained understanding of image content.

8. 2. 7 CNNs for Image Generation

CNNs can generate images by learning patterns and structures from a large dataset. Generative Adversarial Networks (GANs) utilize CNNs to generate compelling images that are indistinguishable from real ones. This exciting application of CNNs has taken creativity and artistic applications to new heights.

8. 2. 8 Transfer Learning with CNNs

Due to the significant amount of computational resources required to train CNNs from scratch, transfer learning has become a popular technique. Transfer learning involves incorporating knowledge from pre-trained CNN models and fine-tuning them for specific tasks. It allows even those without abundant computational resources to utilize the power of CNNs effectively.

8. 2. 9 Limitations and Future Directions

While CNNs have achieved remarkable success, they still have certain limitations. They require a large amount of annotated data for training, and interpreting their decisions can sometimes be challenging. Ongoing research and advancements aim to overcome these limitations and further progress the field of CNNs.

In conclusion, Convolutional Neural Networks (CNNs) have introduced a paradigm shift in image processing tasks. Understanding CNNs' architecture, training process, and applications in image classification, object detection, image segmentation, image generation, and transfer learning allows beginners to dive into the fascinating world of machine learning and computer vision. Remember to keep exploring and experimenting to unleash the true potential of CNNs and push the boundaries of AI in image-related tasks.

8.3 Natural Language Processing (NLP) with Recurrent Networks

8. 3 Natural Language Processing (NLP) with Recurrent Networks

In recent years, Natural Language Processing (NLP) has gained significant attention and popularity due to its ability to enable machines to understand and interpret human language. One of the key techniques used in NLP is the application of Recurrent Neural Networks (RNNs). Captured within this section, we will dive deep into the world of NLP and explore how RNNs are effectively implemented to tackle various language-related tasks.

8. 3. Its primary goal is to enable machines to understand, interpret, and respond to human language in a way that is both meaningful and contextually relevant. NLP finds its applications in various functionalities, including machine translation, sentiment analysis, chatbots, information extraction, and more.

One important aspect of NLP involves understanding language at a deeper level, beyond simple word-for-word matching. This requires the ability to comprehend the meaning, grammar, and structure of sentences, and to infer context from the surrounding words.

8. 3. 2 Recurrent Neural Networks (RNNs)

Recurrent Neural Networks (RNNs) are a class of artificial neural networks that are well-suited for processing sequential data, such as text or speech. Unlike traditional feedforward neural networks, which process input independently, RNNs have a feedback mechanism that allows them to maintain an internal memory of prior inputs.

The key idea behind RNNs is their ability to capture and utilize the temporal dependencies within sequential data. This makes them ideal for language-related tasks as they excel in understanding and generating sequences of words. In the context of NLP, RNN models are trained to understand sentence structure, recognize dependencies between words, predict the next word in a sequence, and perform a variety of other language-related tasks.

8. 3. 3 Long Short-Term Memory (LSTM) Networks

A prevalent architecture used in RNNs for NLP tasks is the Long Short-Term Memory (LSTM) network. LSTMs are designed to address the vanishing and exploding gradient problems typically associated with standard RNNs when processing long sequences.

LSTM networks comprise a memory cell that can remember information over long periods of time, allowing them to capture and utilize long-range dependencies in text. The memory cell can selectively retain or update information, making it particularly effective for processing sequential data. Additionally, LSTM networks consist of input, output, and forget gates that regulate the flow of information, enhancing their ability to handle large or complex textual inputs.

8. 3. 4 Applications of NLP with RNNs

NLP with RNNs finds wide-ranging applications in various industries, reshaping the way we interact with technology. Below are some examples of the tasks that can be accomplished using NLP with RNNs:

1. Sentiment Analysis: RNNs can classify text into positive, negative, or neutral sentiment, allowing businesses to gauge customer sentiment and make informed decisions based on feedback.

2. Machine Translation: NLP-powered RNN models can

automatically translate text from one language to another, significantly facilitating communication between individuals with different languages.

3. Question Answering: RNN models can understand text-based questions and provide relevant answers by extracting and comprehending the necessary information from a given dataset or document.

4. Text Generation: RNNs can be trained on large collections of text data to generate coherent and contextually sound sentences, enabling chatbots or virtual assistants to respond more naturally.

5. Named Entity Recognition: By employing RNNs, it is possible to identify and classify named entities (e. g. , persons, organizations, dates) in a given text, benefiting various applications such as information extraction from news articles or legal documents.

8. 3. 5 Challenges and Future Trends

While NLP with RNNs has made remarkable strides, there are still challenges to overcome. Some common challenges include handling out-of-vocabulary words, extracting meaning from ambiguous sentences, and addressing biases present within training data, among others. Researchers are continually exploring novel architectural improvements, introducing attention mechanisms, or combining RNNs with other techniques to improve performance and address these challenges.

In the future, we can expect more advanced language models that have a deeper understanding of context, nuances, and even emotions associated with human language. Incorporating RNNs with techniques like Transformers will likely lead to more powerful models capable of understanding complex grammatical structures and generating more human-like responses.

8.3.6 Conclusion

Natural Language Processing with Recurrent Networks has revolutionized the way machines interpret and process textual data. RNNs, especially LSTM networks, have proven to be highly effective for tasks involving language comprehension, sequence generation, and more. With ongoing advancements in the field, NLP models are making significant strides toward human-level language understanding and processing. By understanding the fundamental concepts of NLP and RNNs, you can embark on a journey to create sophisticated language models and explore myriad applications that leverage the power of natural language understanding.

8.4 Realworld Applications and Success Stories

8.4 Real-world Applications and Success Stories

Enclosed within this section, we will delve into some real-world applications and success stories of machine learning (ML). In recent years, ML has found extensive implementation across various sectors, transforming industries and revolutionizing the way we live and work. Let's explore some of the remarkable applications and success stories that showcase the power and potential of ML.

1. Healthcare:
ML algorithms have proven to be game-changers in the healthcare industry. In diagnosing diseases, ML models have shown remarkable accuracy, speed, and efficiency. For instance, researchers have developed ML algorithms that analyze medical images, such as X-rays and CT scans, to detect diseases like cancer at an early stage. Additionally, ML-powered systems can predict patient outcomes, help identify high-risk patients, and automate administrative tasks, ensuring better healthcare management.

2. Finance:
The financial sector greatly benefits from ML techniques. ML algorithms can analyze vast amounts of financial data to detect patterns, predict stock market trends, and assist in making investment decisions. Automated fraud detection is another significant application where ML models help identify anomalies and flag suspicious transactions, ensuring better security in financial operations. Furthermore, ML-powered trading systems can analyze market conditions, swiftly execute trades, and perform data-driven risk analysis.

3. Transportation:
ML techniques are reshaping the transportation industry. From self-driving cars to efficient route planning and ride-sharing algorithms, ML is revolutionizing the way we commute. Autonomous vehicles rely heavily on ML models to observe and interpret their surroundings in real-time, making smart decisions to navigate safely. ML algorithms also play a crucial role in improving traffic management, predicting traffic congestion, and optimizing transportation systems.

4. Natural Language Processing:
Another exciting application of ML is natural language processing (NLP), which focuses on enabling machines to understand and communicate in human languages. Virtual assistants like Apple Siri, Amazon Alexa, and Google Assistant showcase the incredible advancements in NLP. These systems employ ML techniques to analyze human speech, recognize patterns, and provide appropriate responses, making them an integral part of our everyday lives.

5. Manufacturing and Supply Chain Management:
ML's potential in manufacturing is immense. ML models are used in predictive maintenance, where they can analyze sensor data to identify potential failures or breakdowns, allowing companies to take proactive measures. Supply chain management greatly benefits from ML algorithms that can optimize inventory, forecast demands, and enhance logistics planning. Through ML, manufacturing processes can become more efficient, reducing costs, improving product quality, and enhancing overall productivity.

6. Agriculture:
The agricultural sector is adopting ML to address various challenges. ML models can analyze data from soil conditions, weather patterns, and crop health sensors to predict optimal irrigation schedules, offer precise nutrient recommendations, and detect diseases or infections in crops. This assists farmers in maximizing yields, reducing the use of pesticides, and increasing

sustainability.

7. Entertainment and Recommendations:
Entertainment platforms leverage ML algorithms to provide highly personalized recommendations to users. Services like Netflix, Spotify, and YouTube curate content based on an individual's viewing or listening history, utilizing ML models to discover patterns and preferences. Moreover, ML-powered recommendation systems help businesses understand user behavior, tailor marketing strategies, and deliver more customized experiences.

8. Astrophysics and Astronomy:
Astrophysics benefits significantly from ML techniques for analyzing vast arrays of astronomical data. ML models assist in categorizing celestial objects, identifying gravitational waves, mapping galaxies, and predicting astronomical events like supernovae or asteroid collisions. By automating data analysis, ML is revolutionizing scientific discoveries and accelerating our understanding of the universe.

These examples just scratch the surface of ML's real-world applications. We could explore numerous others, including image and speech recognition, cybersecurity, energy management, and environmental monitoring, among various fields benefiting from ML techniques.

These success stories illustrate the prowess of ML in transforming entire industries, solving complex problems, and adding significant value to society. As the range and impact of ML continue to expand, the demand for individuals with ML knowledge and skills persists. With this in mind, the importance of understanding the basics of ML becomes increasingly evident, as it paves the way for exciting opportunities and advancements in the years to come.

Chapter 9: Model Deployment Strategies

Model deployment is a critical step in the machine learning lifecycle as it involves making your trained models available for prediction and use in real-world applications. We will discuss various approaches for deploying models, including both traditional and modern methods, along with their advantages and considerations.

1. Local Deployment

Local deployment refers to running and hosting the model on a local machine or server. This strategy is suitable for use cases where the model's predictions are needed within a closed environment, such as a company's intranet or a personal computer. Local deployment allows for quick and easy access to the model without relying on external resources, and it ensures data privacy and security.

However, local deployment has limitations, as it may not scale well for high-demand production systems. It can be resource-intensive and may require manual intervention for maintenance and updates. Additionally, it may lack failover mechanisms or load balancing, which could impact system reliability.

2. Cloud Deployment

Cloud deployment involves deploying machine learning models on cloud-based platforms. Services such as Amazon Web Services (AWS), Google Cloud Platform (GCP), and Microsoft Azure offer tools and infrastructure specifically designed for hosting and running machine learning models. Cloud deployment provides scalability, reliability, and accessibility from anywhere at any time.

With cloud deployment, you can take advantage of auto-scaling capabilities, which automatically adjust the computing resources based on the current demand. This ensures that your model can handle high traffic even during peak times. Additionally, cloud platforms often provide integration with other services like storage, security, and monitoring, simplifying the deployment process.

3. Containerization

Containerization is an increasingly popular technique for deploying machine learning models. It involves bundling the trained model, along with its runtime dependencies and configurations, into a container. Containers provide a lightweight and portable solution, making it easier to deploy models across different environments.

One widely used containerization technology is Docker. By creating a Docker image with your model and its dependencies, you can ensure consistent behavior regardless of the host operating system. Containers also enable easy replication, versioning, and distribution of models, making deployment and collaboration seamless. Additionally, with container orchestrators like Kubernetes, you can manage multiple instances of the model, ensuring high availability and fault tolerance.

4. Serverless Deployment

Serverless deployment is an emerging trend that allows you to deploy machine learning models without worrying about managing servers or infrastructure. Cloud providers such as AWS Lambda, Azure Functions, and Google Cloud Functions offer serverless options where your model is automatically scaled and executed in response to incoming requests.

With serverless deployment, you pay only for the actual resource consumption, making it cost-efficient for low to moderate usage scenarios. It also simplifies deployment and removes the burden of system maintenance. However, serverless deployments may have limitations such as execution time constraints and potential cold start delays, which might impact real-time applications requiring low-latency predictions.

5. Mobile Deployment

Mobile deployment involves embedding your machine learning models on mobile devices, allowing for offline and on-device predictions. This approach is ideal for applications that require real-time predictions without relying on network connectivity or transmitting sensitive data to external servers.

Mobile deployment usually involves model optimization techniques, such as quantization or pruning, to ensure the model's size and computational requirements are manageable on resource-constrained devices. Frameworks like TensorFlow Lite and Core ML provide tools to convert the model into a format suitable for deployment on iOS or Android devices, enabling seamless integration within mobile applications.

Conclusion

Model deployment strategies are diverse and often depend on the specific requirements of your machine learning project. Amidst the information in this chapter, we explored various options, including local deployment, cloud deployment, containerization, serverless deployment, and mobile deployment. Each approach offers its own advantages and considerations.

When choosing a deployment strategy, consider factors such as scalability, maintenance effort, cost, privacy requirements, and real-time performance needs. It is always beneficial to evaluate multiple options and select the one that best aligns with your project's objectives. Remember to keep up with the latest advancements in deployment techniques as the field of machine learning continues to evolve.

9.1 Transitioning from Development to Deployment

When it comes to machine learning, the journey doesn't end with the development of models. The true value of machine learning lies in effectively deploying these models to areas where they can generate insights, improve decision-making processes, and ultimately drive business outcomes. The transition from development to deployment is crucial as it requires careful considerations and a systematic approach. Embedded within this chapter, we will delve into the key aspects and challenges involved in transitioning machine learning models from development to effective deployment.

9.1.1 Understanding the Deployment Pipeline

Before diving into the specifics of transitioning from development to deployment, it is essential to grasp the overall deployment pipeline concept. The deployment pipeline encompasses stages, tools, and processes involved in efficiently and consistently moving your machine learning models from development to production. It includes essential steps like model testing, evaluation, packaging, integration with production systems, and maintenance.

9.1.2 Evaluating Model Performance

The first step towards successful deployment of machine learning models is to thoroughly evaluate their performance. The goal is to assess how well the model generalizes to real-world data and confirms that it meets the required criteria. It includes running the model on a comprehensive testing dataset to understand its accuracy, precision, recall, and other relevant metrics. Conducting comprehensive model evaluation enables you to make informed decisions about the readiness of your model for deployment.

9.1.3 Scaling and Resourcing

While developing and refining machine learning models, you might have utilized a limited dataset or relied on local processing power. However, as you transition to deployment, scalability becomes a major consideration. You need to ensure that your model can handle large datasets, accommodate multiple users or requests, and leverage distributed computing when necessary. Additionally, carefully evaluate the resources required to deploy and maintain the model, such as computational power, storage, and network bandwidth.

9.1.4 Model Packaging and Versioning

To streamline deployment processes and facilitate collaboration among team members, it is important to package your machine learning models effectively. This involves organizing and bundling all the necessary code, dependencies, and trained model parameters into a deployable unit. Consider employing containerization technologies like Docker to encapsulate your models and their required dependencies in a portable manner. Additionally, adopting effective versioning techniques ensures easy tracking of modifications, bug fixes, and enhancements to your models over time.

9.1.5 Integration with Production Systems

Integrating machine learning models with existing production systems can significantly enhance their usability and impact. Whether it is embedding models into web applications, connecting them with enterprise systems, or deploying them in cloud environments, seamless integration is key. You need to identify the appropriate interfaces or APIs to expose your models for operational use. Furthermore, handling issues related to security, authorization, data privacy, and real-time performance becomes critical during integration.

9.1.6 Monitoring and Maintenance

Transitioning from development to deployment necessitates continuous monitoring and maintenance of machine learning models. Once operational, models require regular monitoring to stay on top of performance degradation, concept drift, or other issues that could impact their effectiveness. Building robust monitoring solutions involves logging relevant statistics, setting up alerts for critical events, and establishing feedback loops for continuous improvement. Additionally, establishing maintenance routines to accommodate bug fixes, enhancements, and occasional model retraining is vital.

9.1.7 Risk Management and Governance

While deploying machine learning models, it is important to consider potential risks and establish governance frameworks that ensure ethical, fair, and responsible use of these models. Evaluate potential biases in the training data that might result in undesirable consequences when deployed. Implement measures to understand and mitigate risks associated with model failure or unintended consequences. Establish guidelines to govern the handling of personal data and comply with regulatory requirements.

9.1.8 Addressing Performance Concerns

In some cases, the performance of a machine learning model in a controlled development environment might not translate well in a real-world deployment scenario. The model might face challenges due to variations in the input data distribution, latency constraints, or resource limitations in production environments. Addressing these performance concerns might involve fine-tuning the model, retraining with additional data, adjusting hyperparameters, or implementing more sophisticated algorithms. These iterative improvements are crucial to ensure optimal performance in production environments.

9.1.9 Tracking Deployment Impact

As you complete the transition from development to deployment, it is important to track the impact your machine learning models are having on the intended tasks or applications. Measure and analyze various indicators such as business performance metrics, user feedback, efficiency gains, return on investment, or other relevant indicators. This analysis helps validate the effectiveness of your deployed models and guide future improvements or iterations.

In summary, transitioning from development to deployment involves a systematic approach that goes beyond just codes and models. Evaluating performance, addressing scalability, packaging, integrating with production systems, monitoring, and risk management are some of the key considerations during this phase. By following a comprehensive deployment pipeline and constantly evaluating the impact, you can ensure that your machine learning models are effectively deployed and deliver value to businesses and end-users alike.

9.2 Common Deployment Platforms and Best Practices

Common Deployment Platforms and Best Practices

In the world of machine learning, the ultimate goal is not just to build a successful model, but also to deploy it in a way that allows others to benefit from its capabilities. Deployment platforms provide a framework or infrastructure where your machine learning models can be deployed and used by others in a reliable and scalable manner. Amidst the contents of this section, we will explore common deployment platforms and best practices associated with them.

9.2.1 Cloud Computing Platforms
Cloud computing has revolutionized the field of machine learning deployment by providing scalable compute resources and infrastructure for hosting models. Some of the most widely used cloud computing platforms for machine learning deployment include:

1. Amazon Web Services (AWS): AWS offers a comprehensive suite of machine learning services like Amazon SageMaker and AWS Elastic Beanstalk. These services provide easy-to-use interfaces for model deployment, scaling, and maintenance. AWS also provides serverless options like AWS Lambda that can be used to create serverless machine learning endpoints.

2. Google Cloud Platform (GCP): GCP provides ML-specific services like Google Cloud ML Engine and GCP AI Platform, which enable you to deploy and manage your machine learning models easily. GCP serverless offerings like Cloud Functions and Cloud Run can also be used for deploying models in a serverless manner.

3. Microsoft Azure: Microsoft Azure offers services like Azure Machine Learning and Azure Functions that facilitate deploying and managing machine learning models. Azure Functions, similar to AWS Lambda and Google Cloud Functions are serverless functions that can be used for deploying machine learning models.

These cloud computing platforms provide a range of features, such as auto-scaling, load balancing, and integrated storage options, which make model deployment and management streamlined and efficient. Additionally, they often allow you to integrate with other cloud services like databases, notification systems, and API gateways, further extending the capabilities of your machine learning models.

9.2.2 Containerization Platforms
Containerization is another popular approach for deploying machine learning models. Containers allow you to encapsulate your model, dependencies, and required libraries into a single package, making it easy to deploy consistently across different environments. Some commonly used containerization platforms include:

1. Docker: Docker is a leading platform for building and deploying containers. It provides a lightweight and portable runtime environment that makes it easy to package and distribute machine learning models. Docker containers can be deployed on local machines, cloud platforms, or dedicated container orchestration platforms like Kubernetes.

2. Kubernetes: Kubernetes is an open-source container orchestration platform that automates the deployment, scaling, and management of containerized applications. It provides advanced features like load balancing, service discovery, and self-healing capabilities. Kubernetes, in combination with Docker, is often used for deploying machine learning models at scale.

Containerization platforms offer the advantage of consistent deployment across different environments, simplifying deployment workflows, and making scaling easier. They also ensure that your machine learning models behave consistently, regardless of the underlying infrastructure used.

9.2.3 On-device Deployment
In certain scenarios, deploying machine learning models directly on the device can offer several benefits like reduced latency, improved privacy, and increased offline availability. This approach is particularly relevant for applications like mobile apps, edge computing devices, and Internet of Things (IoT) devices. Some commonly used on-device deployment platforms for machine learning include:

1. TensorFlow Lite: TensorFlow Lite is a lightweight version of TensorFlow, designed specifically for mobile and embedded devices. It allows you to deploy trained TensorFlow models on iOS, Android, and other edge devices.

2. Core ML: Core ML is a framework provided by Apple for integrating machine learning models into iOS, macOS, watchOS, and tvOS applications. It supports popular machine learning frameworks like TensorFlow and PyTorch and provides tools to convert models to the Core ML format.

3. Edge TPU: Edge TPU is an ASIC chip developed by Google, optimized for running TensorFlow Lite models on edge devices. It offers high-performance inferencing at low power, making it ideal for applications in a resource-constrained environment.

On-device deployment platforms offer the advantage of reduced latency and increased privacy since the data processing happens locally on the device, without the need for constant internet connectivity. Additionally, they provide offline availability, allowing users to access the machine learning capabilities even when the internet connection is not available.

Key Best Practices for Model Deployment:

1. Monitoring and Logging: Establish a robust monitoring system to track the performance, usage, and errors encountered during the deployment of your machine learning models. Logging relevant information helps in identifying and resolving issues quickly.

2. Version Control: Employ version control techniques to track changes to your models and their associated artifacts over time. This helps in reverting to the desired version if issues arise and allows for reproducibility.

3. Security Measures: Implement security measures to protect the integrity and confidentiality of your deployed models. Consider encrypting models and applying access controls to prevent unauthorized access and tampering.

4. Scalability: Design models that can scale easily and efficiently on demand. Utilize cloud computing platforms or containerization platforms to allow for automatic scaling based on user demand and the available resources.

5. Testing and Validation: Thoroughly test and validate your models before deployment to ensure that they meet the desired performance standards. Continuous integration and testing practices can help detect any regressions or performance issues.

6. Documentation: Maintain comprehensive documentation that covers all aspects of your deployed models, including how to use them, interpret results, handle failures, and troubleshoot issues. Documentation assists users and future developers in understanding and extending the deployed models.

As you embark on your machine learning deployment journey, it's essential to understand the different platforms available and select the one that best suits your use case. Whether it's a cloud computing platform, a containerization platform, or an on-device deployment approach, following the best practices provided above will help you successfully deploy and manage your machine learning models.

9.3 Scaling Models for Production

Once you have developed a machine learning model that shows promising results, you may want to deploy it in a production environment where it can make real-time predictions or provide valuable data insights. However, successfully scaling your model for production poses its own set of challenges. Housed within this section, we will delve into important considerations and techniques for scaling machine learning models effectively.

1. Infrastructure and computational resources:
When deploying a machine learning model, you need to ensure that the necessary infrastructure and computational resources are available to handle the workload efficiently. This includes selecting and configuring the appropriate hardware, such as GPUs or TPUs, to accelerate the model's performance. Additionally, designing a scalable computational architecture, like using distributed systems or cloud-based platforms, can help handle increased computational demands and provide fault tolerance.

2. Efficient data preprocessing and feature engineering:
As the volume of data increases in a production environment, efficient data preprocessing becomes paramount. Consider streamlining and optimizing your data preprocessing steps to reduce computation time, such as using parallel processing or distributed computing frameworks to handle large-scale data. Similarly, automated feature engineering techniques like deep learning embeddings or dimensionality reduction algorithms can help extract crucial insights from complex data sources swiftly.

3. Scalable model architectures:
To ensure efficient scalability, you may need to reconsider your model architecture choices. Complex models with high computational requirements might need simplification or

streamlining to perform effectively in a production setting. Reducing the model's complexity can enhance its efficiency without compromising on performance. It might also be necessary to decompose the model into multiple sub-models or incorporate ensemble techniques, ensuring parallelization and efficient resource utilization.

4. Load balancing and parallelization:
When serving predictions or processing data in production, it is essential to consider load balancing and parallelization techniques to handle effectively incoming requests. Load balancers distribute the workload across multiple servers or processing units to prevent one component from becoming a bottleneck. Parallelizing tasks using techniques like distributed computing frameworks, asynchronous processing, or multi-threading can significantly improve prediction throughput and reduce latency.

5. Efficient deployment systems:
Developing an efficient deployment system is fundamental to implementing machine learning models in real-world scenarios. Containerization technologies like Docker can help encapsulate your models and dependencies, ensuring reproducibility and portability. Deploying scalable model-serving systems, such as using frameworks like TensorFlow Serving or building REST APIs, ensures easy integration with other applications and effective utilization of computational resources.

6. Continuous integration and automated testing:
Maintaining code quality, reliability, and scalability becomes more crucial as your machine learning models scale in production. Implementing continuous integration pipelines with automated testing frameworks reduces the risk of bugs or regressions. Integration tests can validate the model's performance, ensuring it meets thresholds and complies with expected behavior.

7. Monitoring and performance optimization:
As the deployed machine learning model interacts with real-time

data, monitoring its behavior and performance is of utmost importance. Setting up a robust monitoring system helps identify and resolve issues efficiently. Monitoring metrics such as inference times, resource utilization, prediction accuracy, and error rates are crucial for improving model performance and tuning its hyperparameters to achieve optimal results.

8. Data privacy and security considerations:
Scaling machine learning models for production also entails handling user data ethically and following appropriate security measures. Ensuring compliance with applicable regulations and industry standards regarding data privacy and protection should be integrated into the development and deployment pipeline. Techniques such as encryption or anonymization can help safeguard sensitive information processed by the model.

9. Continuous improvement and model maintenance:
Deploying a machine learning model in production is not a one-time task; it requires continuous improvement and maintenance. Evaluating model performance, retraining the model periodically with fresh data, and updating its underlying infrastructure and dependencies are crucial to keeping the system efficient and reliable over time.

Scaling machine learning models for production involves an intricate blend of technical expertise, architectural design, and domain-specific considerations. By carefully addressing each aspect discussed in this section, you will arrive at a well-designed and efficient production system that can handle increasing workloads, adapt to changing data dynamics, and effectively provide meaningful predictions or insights.

9.4 Continuous Monitoring and Maintenance Strategies

Machine learning models, once deployed in production, need consistent monitoring and maintenance to ensure optimal performance and accurate results over time. Continuous monitoring and maintenance strategies are essential aspects of machine learning lifecycle management, enabling organizations to detect and address any performance issues or drift that may occur as the data distribution evolves. Embedded within this section, we will discuss the importance of continuous monitoring and various strategies to effectively maintain machine learning models.

9.4.1 Importance of Continuous Monitoring

Continuous monitoring serves as a crucial component of machine learning deployment, as it allows organizations to keep track of their models' performance, ensure they operate as intended, and detect potential issues promptly. Without ongoing monitoring, even the most accurate and efficient models may deteriorate over time due to various reasons, including changing user behavior, shifts in the data distribution, or emerging external factors.

By continuously monitoring a machine learning model, organizations can detect anomalies, evaluate predictive performance, and take the necessary corrective measures. Proactive monitoring helps ensure that models meet predefined performance standards, adhere to compliance regulations, and deliver reliable insights and predictions.

9.4.2 Data Quality Monitoring

One fundamental aspect of continuous monitoring relates to data quality. As machine learning models depend heavily on training data, detecting and addressing data quality issues are of paramount importance. Common data quality challenges include missing values, outliers, inconsistencies, and skewed distributions.

Organizations must establish a robust data quality monitoring system to identify various data anomalies. This can involve setting up data pipelines that validate input data, perform statistical checks, and compare incoming data with predefined benchmarks. Data quality monitoring helps mitigate biases and reduces the risk of any critical decisions made based on erroneous or misleading inputs.

9.4.3 Performance Monitoring

Monitoring the performance of a machine learning model is another crucial aspect of continuous maintenance. Performance metrics, such as accuracy, precision, recall, or F1-score, should be tracked regularly to evaluate and ensure the model's reliability. Additionally, organizations may need to define domain-specific metrics that measure performance in relation to specific business requirements.

Performance monitoring can involve monitoring time-series prediction accuracy or conducting A/B tests using holdout datasets. By comparing the model's predictions with ground truth labels or live feedback, organizations can identify any performance degradation, detect overfitting, or uncover issues caused by changes in the data distribution.

9.4.4 Retraining and Model Updating

As models operate in dynamic environments, it is crucial to retrain or update them periodically to maintain accuracy and efficacy. Monitoring plays a critical role in alerting organizations when it is time to retrain or update a model.

Retraining can follow a structured approach with fixed time intervals or a more dynamic strategy based on performance degradation or shifts in data characteristics. Retraining involves accumulating new labeled data, creating a new model version, and deploying it seamlessly into the production environment. Depending on the scale and model complexity, retraining may require automated pipelines or involve specialized tools and frameworks.

Model updating refers to the process of incorporating new knowledge or domain expertise into a trained model to enhance its performance. It can involve fine-tuning specific model parameters, incorporating additional training data, or leveraging transfer learning techniques. This process ensures that the model remains up to date and aligned with the evolving problem domain.

9.4.5 Bias and Fairness Monitoring

Monitoring for biases and ensuring fairness in machine learning models is an integral part of ethical AI. Biases can arise from both historical data and imbalances in the representation of certain groups within the training data. These biases can lead to unfair decisions or reinforce existing societal inequalities.

To address bias and fairness concerns, organizations should implement regular checks to identify discriminatory behavior of their models. Techniques such as fairness metrics, demographic parity analysis, and equalized odds assessment can uncover potential discrimination patterns. If any biases are detected, organizations must consult domain experts to understand the underlying causes and take corrective actions to mitigate these biases.

9.4.6 Collaboration between Data Science and Operations Teams

Successful continuous monitoring and maintenance require effective collaboration between data science and operations teams. Data scientists and machine learning engineers should work closely with DevOps or SRE (Site Reliability Engineering) teams to deploy models and establish robust monitoring and maintenance pipelines.

Regular communication and collaboration throughout the lifecycle ensure that operational inputs and requirements are considered when designing monitoring strategies. Data scientists need to collaborate with operations teams to understand the production environment's limitations, resource availability, and establish suitable monitoring infrastructure to continuously analyze model performance.

In summary, continuous monitoring and maintenance are essential aspects of successful machine learning model deployments. By monitoring the data quality, performance, biases, and fairness of the models, organizations can identify and rectify potential issues promptly. Additionally, establishing effective collaboration between data science and operations teams allows for seamless implementation of proper monitoring pipelines. Continuously enhancing and refining machine learning models results in improved reliability, delivering accurate and actionable insights to solve real-world problems effectively.

Chapter 10: Ethical Considerations in Machine Learning

Ethical Considerations in Machine Learning
Machine learning has become an integral part of our lives, transforming various industries and enhancing our daily experiences. However, as we delve deeper into this field, it is important to reflect on the ethical implications that arise from adopting and implementing machine learning systems. Entailed within this chapter, we will explore the ethical considerations surrounding machine learning and how they can affect individuals, societies, and the overall functioning of AI-based systems.

1. Bias and Fairness:
One of the most critical ethical aspects in machine learning is the presence of bias in data and algorithms. Machine learning models are trained using historical data, which can unintentionally perpetuate existing biases and discrimination present in society. This bias can lead to discriminatory practices, resulting in disparate outcomes for individuals based on characteristics such as gender, race, or socioeconomic status. As machine learning practitioners, it is crucial to address and mitigate bias through various methods, including diverse and representative datasets, fairness metrics, and bias-checking tools.

2. Privacy and Data Security:
Machine learning systems often rely on extensive datasets, including personal information and sensitive data. Privacy concerns may arise when handling such data, which can be exploited or misused if not adequately protected. This chapter will examine ethical guidelines for data collection, storage, and usage, highlighting the importance of anonymization, data

encryption, and informed consent. Additionally, we will explore emerging frameworks such as differential privacy that aim to strike a balance between data utility and individual privacy.

3. Transparency and Explainability:
Machine learning models are often regarded as black boxes due to their complex nature, making it challenging to understand their decision-making processes. However, with the increasing reliance on AI systems, it becomes crucial to ensure transparency and explainability. Users should have insight into why an AI system produced a particular output or decision, especially in critical domains such as healthcare or criminal justice. This chapter will discuss various techniques, such as model interpretability, rule extraction, and visualizations, which can help make machine learning systems more transparent and accountable.

4. Social Implications:
Machine learning algorithms have the potential to impact societal and cultural norms, both positively and negatively. This section of the chapter will delve into issues like employment, economics, and power disparities. We will explore the challenges posed by automation, job displacement, and the concentration of power among those who have access to and control over AI technologies. Understanding and addressing these ethical considerations are essential to ensure a fair and inclusive future, where the benefits of machine learning are equitably distributed.

5. Accountability and Governance:
As machine learning plays an increasing role in critical decision-making processes, it is vital to establish accountability and governance frameworks. This chapter will examine the need for clear regulations, ethical guidelines, and audit mechanisms to monitor the deployment and usage of machine learning systems. We will delve into the key stakeholders involved, including developers, policymakers, and society as a whole, emphasizing the shared responsibility in aligning machine learning practices with ethical standards.

6. Mitigating Malicious Use:
Lastly, we will discuss the ethical considerations surrounding the potential misuse and harmful applications of machine learning. We will explore the risks associated with deepfakes, misinformation, algorithmic manipulation, and autonomous weapons. This section will underline the importance of responsible development and deployment of machine learning, where ethical considerations should be at the forefront to prevent societal harm.

Conclusion:
While machine learning promises tremendous advancements and benefits, it is crucial to approach its design, development, and deployment with the utmost consideration for ethical principles. This chapter notably emphasizes the role of bias mitigation, privacy protection, transparency, fairness, and accountability in influencing the ethical direction of machine learning systems. It is only by proactively addressing these ethical considerations that we can ensure the responsible and justified use of AI technologies, fostering ethical choices that lead to positive societal impact and long-term sustainability.

10.1 Navigating Ethical Challenges in ML

Machine Learning (ML) has rapidly transformed various aspects of our lives, from personalized recommendations on online platforms to autonomous vehicles. However, as this technology becomes more prevalent, it brings along ethical challenges that need careful consideration. Enclosed within this section, we will explore these challenges and discuss how to navigate them responsibly.

1. Bias in ML: One crucial ethical consideration in ML is the existence of bias in algorithms. Bias can emerge due to biased training data, leading to unequal treatment or unfair outcomes for individuals or groups. As beginners, it's essential to recognize and address bias during the entire ML lifecycle, starting from data collection, preprocessing, model development, and even deployment. Regularly evaluate your models for bias, interpret the results, and take corrective actions if necessary.

2. Data Privacy and Security: ML models often require extensive data to train and make accurate predictions. However, the collection and usage of personal and sensitive data raise concerns regarding privacy and security. Beginners should prioritize privacy by adopting appropriate data anonymization techniques, including data encryption and secure protocols for data transmission. Complying with relevant privacy regulations, obtaining user consent, and ensuring secure storage and retrieval of data should be integral parts of your ML workflow.

3. Transparency and Explainability: As ML algorithms become more complex, they may seem like black boxes, making it difficult to understand how decisions are made. However, understanding the underlying logic is crucial to ensure fairness

and accountability. Beginners should aim for transparency and explainability in their ML models. Utilize interpretable models, provide explanations for predictions, and document the decision-making process in order to improve transparency and facilitate user trust.

4. Adversarial Attacks: Adversarial attacks refer to manipulating ML models by introducing malicious inputs in order to deceive, mislead, or exploit the system. As a beginner, it's important to be aware of such attacks and take preventive measures. Employ techniques like adversarial training to enhance model resilience against such attacks. Regularly evaluate your models for vulnerabilities and stay up to date with the latest research on adversarial robustness.

5. Job Displacement: ML technology has the potential to automate tasks traditionally performed by humans, leading to concerns about job displacement. As an ML practitioner, it is essential to consider and anticipate these social and economic impacts. Understanding the potential consequences and developing strategies to mitigate them, such as retraining/upskilling affected individuals or incorporating human oversight in automated systems, helps ensure responsible deployment of ML technology.

6. Throughput Bias and Social Impact: Certain ML applications, such as facial recognition systems or predictive policing algorithms, can disproportionately impact specific social groups, perpetuate existing biases, or result in unfair outcomes. Beginners must identify and confront the ethical challenges surrounding the social impact of ML systems. Engage with the affected communities, consult domain experts, validate the robustness of your models concerning various demographic groups, and iterate on your development process to minimize potential biases.

7. Environmental Impact: ML models often consume significant computational resources, contributing to increased energy consumption and carbon footprint. As an AI practitioner, you

should consider the ecological impact of both model development and deployment processes. Using energy-efficient hardware, optimizing model architectures, and exploring techniques like quantization or knowledge distillation can help reduce the environmental footprint of machine learning systems.

8. Intellectual Property and Reproducibility: ML research and development rely on open sharing of knowledge and collaboration. However, some ethical concerns arise, including intellectual property rights, equitable access to technology, and reproducibility of results. Beginner practitioners must adhere to open science practices, including sharing code, datasets, and techniques whenever possible. Respect intellectual property rights and promote an inclusive environment that fosters collaboration and knowledge dissemination within the ML community.

9. Continuous Learning and Adaptation: The ethical journey in ML doesn't end once a model is deployed. Models need continuous learning and adaptation to the changing demands of their applications. This presents ethical challenges, including data retention, ongoing bias evaluation, and maintaining trust within automated systems. Stay vigilant, monitor your models' performance and impact, and be prepared to update your models based on new datasets or evolving ethical guidelines.

10. Collaboration and Dialogue: Lastly, navigating ethical challenges in ML requires collaboration among various stakeholders, including researchers, practitioners, policymakers, and end-users. Engage in open and inclusive discussions, participate in forums, workshops, and conferences, and contribute to the development of industry and community standards. Establish a supportive network that encourages ethical ML practices and fosters an environment for responsible AI development.

By understanding and actively navigating the ethical challenges in ML, beginners can ethically harness this powerful technology while minimizing potential harms. Embracing a proactive and responsible approach to machine learning not only enhances the fairness and effectiveness of your models but also contributes to a more ethical and inclusive AI ecosystem.

10.2 Addressing Bias and Fairness in Algorithms

In the pursuit of creating efficient and effective algorithms, it is crucial to address the issues of bias and fairness that may arise during the development and implementation of machine learning models. Bias can manifest in various ways, such as favoring particular groups or discriminating against certain demographics, potentially leading to undesired outcomes and perpetuating social inequalities. Therefore, it is imperative to pay close attention to addressing bias and ensuring fairness in the algorithms we create. Amidst these section, we will delve into strategies and techniques that can be employed to mitigate bias and promote fairness within machine learning algorithms.

1. Defining Bias and Fairness:
Before we dive into addressing bias and fairness, let us establish a common understanding of these terms. Bias, in the context of machine learning algorithms, refers to any systematic favoritism or prejudice shown by the model towards specific groups or attributes. Fairness, on the other hand, implies equal treatment and predictive outcomes across different groups, ensuring that unintended discrimination does not influence the algorithm's decisions.

2. Data Preprocessing:
Addressing bias and promoting fairness begins with the quality and composition of the training data. Careful data preprocessing is necessary to identify any biases present in the dataset. Analyzing the data for representation imbalances or discrepancies and correcting them through techniques such as resampling or data augmentation can help in aligning the model's training process with real-world fairness concerns.

3. Considering Protected Characteristics:
Protected characteristics, such as race, gender, age, or religion, must be taken into account while assessing fairness within machine learning algorithms. Understanding which attributes require special consideration is crucial, as models may unknowingly rely on these protected characteristics during the decision-making process, leading to biased outcomes. By explicitly addressing this issue and designing algorithms that decouple the reliance on protected attributes from decision-making, the potential for biased behavior can be significantly reduced.

4. Exploring Multiple Fairness Metrics:
Fairness cannot be measured by a single metric, and different fairness notions may exist depending upon the problem domain and stakeholders' perspectives. It is recommended to adopt multiple fairness metrics to evaluate the performance of the algorithm across various dimensions. These metrics can include statistical parity, equalized odds, and demographic parity, among others. By comparing and analyzing the algorithm's fairness performance using multiple metrics, a more comprehensive assessment of fairness can be achieved.

5. Regularization Techniques:
Bias and fairness constraints can be explicitly incorporated into the learning process using regularization techniques. Regularization methods like fairness-aware learning, which aim to optimize not only accuracy but fairness as well, can help strike a balance between the two objectives during model training.

6. Transparency and Explainability:
Addressing bias and ensuring fairness in algorithms requires transparency and explainability. Models should be designed with interpretable mechanisms that allow us to uncover the reasons behind particular decisions and identify potential sources of bias. Techniques like rule-based classifiers and model-agnostic interpretability methods can be employed to gain insights and understand the decision-making process of the algorithm.

7. Post-processing and Algorithmic Adjustments:
After the initial training phase, post-processing techniques can be employed to further promote fairness within the algorithm. These techniques involve adjusting the outputs of the model to satisfy certain fairness constraints. For instance, a calibration process can be applied to ensure fair classification outcomes across different groups, minimizing any disparities caused by inherent biases within the learned model.

8. Feedback Loop and Continuous Monitoring:
Addressing bias and fairness is an ongoing process that requires continuous monitoring and feedback from affected stakeholders and communities. Implementing feedback loops that involve regular auditing and incorporating external input can help uncover biases that may not have been addressed in the initial model development phase. Continuously iterating on the algorithm based on this feedback can correct any bias or unfairness that is discovered.

9. Ethical Considerations:
Lastly, it is vital to recognize the ethical responsibilities of AI practitioners and developers in mitigating bias and ensuring fairness. As creators and custodians of these algorithms, it is our duty to be mindful of ethical considerations, actively questioning and minimizing any potential harms that may arise from biased or less fair algorithms. Incorporating diverse perspectives and involving multidisciplinary teams in the algorithm development process can foster critical thinking and lead to more fair and balanced outcomes.

Addressing bias and promoting fairness in algorithms is an ongoing challenge that requires the combined efforts of researchers, developers, policy-makers, and users alike. By incorporating techniques from data preprocessing and algorithm design to transparency and regular feedback loops, it is possible to minimize bias and strive for fairness in machine learning algorithms. Through this holistic approach, we can ensure that algorithms do not perpetuate social inequalities and contribute positively to a fair and inclusive society.

10.3 Ensuring Transparency and Accountability

In the world of machine learning, transparency and accountability are crucial aspects that must be upheld to ensure the ethical and responsible implementation of algorithms. As machine learning models become increasingly pervasive in various domains, it is essential for developers and users alike to prioritize transparency and accountability to build trust and mitigate potential risks.

1. The Importance of Transparency:
Transparency refers to the extent to which the inner workings of machine learning models can be understood by humans. In order to ensure transparency, it is necessary to provide clear documentation and detailed explanations of the algorithms used, along with the data sources employed during the model's creation. Transparency enables developers and stakeholders to comprehend how decisions are made by the algorithm, thereby promoting an understanding of potential biases or shortcomings.

2. Addressing Bias and Fairness:
One of the major concerns in machine learning is the presence of biased decisions that can result from algorithms being trained on biased or incomplete data. To ensure fairness, it is crucial to identify and address biases present in the data used for training, as well as in the design and implementation of the machine learning model. Regularly examining and monitoring the outputs of a model for unintended biases is an ethical responsibility that must not be overlooked.

3. Ethical Considerations:
Transparency goes hand in hand with ensuring ethical

considerations within machine learning systems. Developers should refrain from using data that is obtained unethically or without proper consent, and should also consider potential negative impacts on individuals or communities that could arise from their models. Establishing ethical guidelines and fostering an open dialogue regarding the ethical dimensions of machine learning are effective ways to enhance transparency and accountability.

4. Explainability and Interpretability:
Another aspect of transparency involves making machine learning models interpretable and explainable. Given the complexity of many algorithms, it is often challenging for non-experts to understand why a certain. decision is made. Techniques such as "model-agnostic" explanation approaches, utilizing methods like feature importance analysis or generating simple rule-based explanations, can assist in explaining and interpreting the decisions made by a machine learning model. This promotes accountability by enabling stakeholders to understand and address any shortcomings or biases in the system.

5. Open-Source and Collaboration:
Open-source initiatives and collaboration initiatives play a vital role in ensuring transparency. By sharing code, data, and methodologies, developers can foster accountability and scrutiny from the wider community. This approach also encourages peer review and robust testing, leading to more reliable, accurate, and transparent machine learning systems.

6. Auditing and Impact Assessment:
Regular audits and impact assessments should be conducted to evaluate the performance, fairness, and unintended consequences of machine learning models. These evaluations can aid in identifying biases and ensure compliance with regulations and ethical guidelines. Implementing measures to track and monitor the usage of models further strengthens accountability while fostering a data-driven culture that recognizes continuous improvement.

7. Accountability with Privacy Considerations:
Transparency should not be at the expense of privacy protection. User privacy is of paramount importance, and models should be designed and deployed with privacy safeguards in place. Employing techniques like differential privacy or federated learning can prevent the disclosure of sensitive information while still maintaining transparency and accountability.

8. Responsible Data Collection and Management:
To ensure transparency and accountability, collecting high-quality and unbiased data is crucial. Rigorous data collection practices, such as avoiding biased sampling or data extraction, as well as ensuring proper data anonymization and security, are essential for responsible development and deployment of machine learning systems.

In conclusion, transparency and accountability are fundamental pillars of responsible machine learning. Approaching transparency systematically includes addressing biases, ethical considerations, explainability, open-source collaboration, auditing, and privacy protection. These practices enable developers, users, and societies at large to understand, critique, and improve machine learning models, thereby ensuring their responsible and fair adoption.

10.4 Legal and Ethical Implications in Model Deployment

When it comes to deploying machine learning models, it is imperative to consider the legal and ethical implications surrounding the use of these models. As AI technology continues to advance and integrate into various industries, it becomes crucial to ensure that models are deployed in a responsible and ethical manner to avoid potential harm and misuse. Embraced by this section, we will explore some important legal and ethical considerations that should be taken into account during the model deployment process.

1. Bias and Fairness:
One of the primary concerns in machine learning is the potential for bias in the data or in the model itself. Biased data can lead to unfair outcomes, discrimination, and perpetuation of existing biases. It is essential to thoroughly analyze the data used in training the model for any biases and take appropriate measures to mitigate them. Additionally, fairness metrics should be established to evaluate the performance of the model and address any discriminatory behavior.

2. Privacy and Data Protection:
The deployment of machine learning models often involves dealing with sensitive data such as personal information, financial records, or healthcare data. It is crucial to handle this data with the utmost care and adhere to privacy and data protection regulations. Organizations must obtain explicit consent for collecting, storing, and using personal data. Anonymization techniques and strong data security practices should be employed to mitigate the risk of data breaches and unauthorized access.

3. Transparency and Explainability:
Machine learning models are often considered to be black boxes, making it challenging to understand how they arrive at their decisions. However, it is important to strive for model explainability, especially in critical domains such as healthcare and finance. Deployed models should be interpretable, allowing stakeholders and end-users to understand the factors influencing predictions and decisions. Explaining and justifying the model's behavior not only helps build trust but can also identify potential biases or errors.

4. Intellectual Property Rights:
Models that are deployed for commercial purposes should respect intellectual property rights. Developers must ensure that they have the necessary licensing or permissions for algorithms, datasets, or any third-party components used in the development of the model. Additionally, organizations need to consider the implications of intellectual property rights when collaborating or sharing models with other entities.

5. Accountability and Liability:
When AI models are deployed in critical domains such as healthcare or autonomous driving, the issue of accountability and liability arises. It is important to clearly define roles and responsibilities to determine who should be held accountable for the decisions made by the model. Discussing the legal frameworks and ethical guidelines that govern model deployment can help build accountability and allocate responsibilities appropriately.

6. Impact on Employment and Society:
Deployment of AI models undoubtedly has the potential to transform industries and automate various tasks. While this has clear benefits in terms of efficiency and productivity, it is essential to consider the impact on employment and society as a whole. As certain jobs become automated, new employment opportunities may arise, but there could also be significant social and economic implications. Careful consideration should be given to strategies and policies aimed at minimizing the negative

effects of technological advancements.

7. Continuous Monitoring and Iteration:
Machine learning models are not a one-time development but require continuous monitoring and iteration. Regularly evaluating the model's performance, addressing any biases or ethical concerns, and keeping up with legal and regulatory changes is crucial. Organizations should establish robust model governance frameworks and compliance procedures to ensure the ongoing legality, ethics, and quality of the deployed models.

In conclusion, model deployment goes beyond technical considerations and requires an understanding of the legal and ethical implications surrounding AI systems. Addressing bias, privacy, transparency, intellectual property rights, accountability, and societal impact are vital for responsible and ethical deployment. Organizations and developers must prioritize these considerations to build trust, ensure fairness, and mitigate potential harm to individuals and society as a whole.

Chapter 11: Resources for Continuous Learning

Resources for Continuous Learning

As the field of AI continues to evolve rapidly, it's important to cultivate a habit of continuous learning and stay up to date with the latest developments. This chapter aims to provide you with a curated list of valuable resources that can further enhance your knowledge and support your lifelong learning journey.

1. Online Courses:
- Coursera: Coursera offers a wide range of machine learning and AI courses, including the renowned "Machine Learning" course by Andrew Ng. These courses provide comprehensive and in-depth knowledge, suitable for beginners as well as advanced learners.
- edX: edX features courses from prestigious universities such as MIT and Harvard. Their machine learning courses cover both fundamentals and real-world applications, making it an excellent supplement to your learning.
- Udacity: Udacity offers specialized nanodegree programs focused on machine learning and AI. Designed by industry professionals, these courses provide hands-on experience and help bridge the gap between theory and practice.

2. Books:
- "Pattern Recognition and Machine Learning" by Christopher M. Bishop: This book covers a vast range of topics with a focus on pattern recognition and statistical learning techniques. It combines theoretical concepts with practical applications and is suitable for readers with a mathematical background.
- "Hands-On Machine Learning with Scikit-Learn, Keras, and TensorFlow" by Aurélien Géron: This book enables you to dive

into real-world projects, using popular libraries like Scikit-Learn, Keras, and TensorFlow. It provides hands-on examples and encourages experimenting with various ML algorithms.
- "Deep Learning" by Ian Goodfellow, Yoshua Bengio, and Aaron Courville: This book is an in-depth exploration of deep learning techniques. It covers both the theoretical foundations and practical aspects of building and training neural networks.

3. Online Platforms and Communities:
- Kaggle: Kaggle is a platform for data science and machine learning practitioners. It hosts various competitions, where you can participate, learn from others, and improve your skills through practice. Kaggle also provides datasets and kernels that offer valuable insights into real-world machine learning problems.
- GitHub: GitHub is a code repository platform where you can find numerous open-source machine learning projects. Exploring these projects and studying their implementation details can deepen your understanding and expose you to the latest cutting-edge techniques in the field.
- Reddit: The subreddit r/MachineLearning serves as a vibrant community for machine learning enthusiasts. Here, you can find relevant discussions, insightful articles, and stay up to date with the latest trends. Other subreddits like r/LearnMachineLearning and r/MLQuestions are also great for seeking guidance and clarifying doubts.

4. Conferences and Workshops:
- NeurIPS: The Conference on Neural Information Processing Systems is the leading machine learning and computational neuroscience conference. It features tutorials, workshops, keynote lectures, and paper presentations from leading researchers around the globe.
- International Conference on Machine Learning (ICML): ICML is a premier machine learning conference that covers a wide array of topics. It includes workshops, tutorials, and paper presentations, showcasing cutting-edge machine learning research.
- TensorFlow Dev Summit: This annual event focuses on

Google's TensorFlow framework. It provides insights into the latest features, tools, and best practices, making it an excellent opportunity for both beginners and advanced practitioners to keep up with TensorFlow's advancements.

5. Blogs and Newsletters:
- Towards Data Science: Towards Data Science is a platform that hosts a vast collection of articles and tutorials contributed by the machine learning community. It covers various topics, ranging from introductory concepts to advanced techniques, across both theory and practice.
- Medium machine learning publications: Medium hosts several machine learning publications, such as "Towards Data Science" and "The Startup." These publications offer a wide range of articles written by industry experts, providing practical tips, code tutorials, and insights into emerging trends.
- OpenAI: OpenAI's blog publishes regular articles highlighting their research findings and advancements in AI technologies. Reading these articles can broaden your perspective and keep you informed about the latest breakthroughs.

Remember, the field of machine learning is vast and ever-evolving. It is essential to invest time in continuous learning, exploring various resources, building practical projects, and actively engaging with the machine learning community. Embrace the learning journey, stay curious, and be open to new ideas. Good luck on your path to becoming an accomplished machine learning practitioner!

11.1 Recommended Books, Courses, and Online Platforms

11. 1 Recommended Books, Courses, and Online Platforms

When delving into the vast and fascinating field of machine learning, it's crucial to equip yourself with the right knowledge and resources to ensure a strong foundation. Engulfed by this section of the book, we will discuss various recommended books, courses, and online platforms that can greatly assist beginners in understanding and mastering the concepts of machine learning.

11. 1. 1 Recommended Books

Books have been a timeless medium for comprehensive learning. Here are a few highly regarded books geared towards beginners in machine learning:

1. "Hands-On Machine Learning with Scikit-Learn, Keras, and TensorFlow: Concepts, Tools, and Techniques to Build Intelligent Systems" by Aurélien Géron: This book takes a practical approach, providing hands-on examples and illustrating machine learning techniques using Python libraries, including Scikit-Learn, Keras, and TensorFlow.

2. "Machine Learning Yearning" by Andrew Ng: From one of the most reputable figures in the field, this book offers valuable insights into practical aspects of machine learning and provides an informal advice-type format, helping beginners navigate challenges.

3. "Introduction to Machine Learning with Python: A Guide for Data Scientists" by Andreas C. Müller and Sarah Guido: This book takes a step-by-step approach to understanding machine

learning fundamentals using Python. It covers important topics like classification, regression, dimensionality reduction, and more.

4. "Pattern Recognition and Machine Learning" by Christopher M. Bishop: For those seeking a deeper mathematical understanding, Bishop's book is highly recommended. It covers a wide range of topics including Bayesian methods, graphical models, and neural networks.

11.1.2 Recommended Courses

Courses provide a structured and interactive learning experience. There are numerous online platforms offering machine learning courses, but here are a few highly recommended ones:

1. Coursera: Known for its high-quality courses, Coursera offers a vast range of machine learning courses. Standout options include "Machine Learning" by Andrew Ng and "Applied Data Science with Python" specialization.

2. edX: Another reputable online learning platform that offers a variety of machine learning courses. Standout options include "Introduction to Artificial Intelligence" by IBM and "Deep Learning Fundamentals" by Microsoft.

3. Udacity: This platform provides self-paced nanodegree programs extensively covering machine learning topics. It includes "Intro to Machine Learning with PyTorch" and "Machine Learning Engineer Nanodegree."

4. Stanford University's CS229: For an in-depth understanding, you can access course materials and lectures online. This course covers a wide range of machine learning topics and is helpful for individuals seeking a rigorous academic experience.

11.1.3 Recommended Online Platforms

To supplement your learning journey, online platforms dedicated to machine learning provide additional resources, practice problems, and real-world application scenarios. Here are a few recommended platforms:

1. Kaggle: A platform that enables users to solve various real-world machine learning problems, access datasets for practicing, and participate in competitions to enhance their skills.

2. TensorFlow official website: TensorFlow, an open-source machine learning library, offers extensive documentation, tutorials, and code examples suitable for beginners as well as advanced users.

3. scikit-learn documentation: Scikit-learn, another popular machine learning library, provides comprehensive documentation including user guides, API references, and tutorials to help users navigate the library effectively.

4. GitHub: Utilize repositories on GitHub to explore and access open-source machine learning projects, codes, and resources shared by the machine learning community. This will enable you to learn from others and contribute to the open-source development ecosystem.

By utilizing the books, courses, and online platforms mentioned above, beginners can gain a strong understanding of machine learning concepts while building their practical skills. Remember that a combination of theoretical knowledge, hands-on practice, and exploration of real-world datasets will help solidify your understanding and proficiency in machine learning.

11.2 Engaging with the Machine Learning Community

Embarking on a journey into the fascinating world of machine learning can often be a daunting task for beginners. While it is certainly possible to learn the theoretical aspects of machine learning on your own, actively engaging and becoming a part of the machine learning community can greatly accelerate your learning and provide you with invaluable support.

The machine learning community is a global network of experts, researchers, students, and enthusiasts who are collectively working towards advancing the field. Engaging with this community involves actively participating in discussions, attending conferences, joining online forums, and collaborating on projects. Here, we will explore several ways in which you can engage with the machine learning community and dive deeper into the world of this powerful technology.

1. Attend Conferences and Meetups: Machine learning conferences, such as the International Conference on Machine Learning (ICML), NeurIPS, or specialized conferences like ACL or AAAI, bring together leading researchers and practitioners from around the world. Attending these events allows you to learn about the latest research breakthroughs, network with experts, and gain valuable insights into the field. Additionally, local meetups focusing on machine learning often provide beginner-friendly environments for learning and networking.

2. Join Online Communities: The internet is teeming with online communities dedicated to machine learning where you can engage with like-minded individuals, ask questions, and learn from experts. The most popular platforms include forums such as Reddit's r/MachineLearning and Stack Exchange's Cross

Validated. Participating regularly in these communities will expose you to diverse perspectives and help foster your understanding of the various complexities of machine learning.

3. Learn by Doing: Machine learning challenges and competitions organized by platforms like Kaggle, DrivenData, or AI competitions foster a sense of healthy competition and provide opportunities to learn and showcase your skills. By participating in these challenges, you not only develop real-world problem-solving skills but also have the chance to engage with other participants and receive valuable feedback on your methods.

4. Follow Machine Learning Blogs: Numerous experts and researchers maintain their own blogs, where they share knowledge, experiences, and updated information on cutting-edge techniques. Some prominent sources include Distill, Towards Data Science, or the blogs of prominent AI research organizations like OpenAI and Google AI. Regularly reading these blogs will keep you up-to-date with the latest trends and developments in machine learning.

5. Collaborate on Open-Source Projects: An excellent way to engage with the machine learning community is by contributing to open-source projects. Platforms like GitHub host countless machine learning repositories that cover a wide range of topics and projects. By contributing to these projects, you can both learn from others' work and gain public recognition, which serves to strengthen your presence within the community.

6. Engage in Research and Publications: As you advance in your understanding of machine learning, you might want to actively contribute to research in the field. Attend conferences that accept poster or paper submissions and seek feedback from experts. Publishing your research findings not only showcases your work but also enables you to receive valuable feedback and opens the door to collaboration opportunities.

7. Join Research and Study Groups: Study groups provide a

supportive environment for exploring machine learning concepts and seeking explanations to complex topics. They may involve collaborative discussions, practical coding sessions, or journal clubs where participants analyze scientific papers together. Engaging in such groups not only helps solidify your understanding but also fosters camaraderie within the community.

8. Contribute to Educational Initiatives: As you progress in your machine learning journey, consider giving back to the community by contributing to educational initiatives. Participate in forums to help answer questions from beginners or create educational content to help aspiring learners. Volunteering your knowledge and expertise not only enhances your own understanding but also helps others embarking on their machine learning voyage.

Engaging with the machine learning community is an ongoing process and demands dedication, perseverance, and continuous learning. By immersing yourself in this vibrant network of like-minded individuals, you will gain deeper insights, boost your learning curve, and become an active participant in shaping the future of machine learning. Remember to approach each interaction with curiosity, humility, and a spirit of collaboration, for it is through shared knowledge that the field continues to flourish.

11.3 Participating in Conferences and Workshops

Conferences and workshops play a vital role in the field of machine learning, offering valuable opportunities for learning, networking, and disseminating research findings. As a beginner in the field, attending these events can greatly enhance your understanding and provide you with crucial exposure to current trends and advancements in machine learning.

1. Importance of Conferences and Workshops:
Conferences and workshops serve as platforms where researchers, professionals, and enthusiasts from academia and industry come together to share knowledge, present new research findings, discuss challenges, and explore potential collaborations. These events feature keynote speeches, sessions with paper presentations, poster sessions, panel discussions, and various interactive activities. By participating in these gatherings, you will be able to interact with experts, gaining exposure to cutting-edge research, enhancing your knowledge, and widening your professional network.

2. Finding the Right Conferences and Workshops:
As a beginner, it might be overwhelming to decide which conferences and workshops to attend. Start by identifying well-established conferences related to machine learning and artificial intelligence, such as NeurIPS (Conference on Neural Information Processing Systems), ICML (International Conference on Machine Learning), or ICLR (International Conference on Learning Representations). Additionally, explore more specialized workshops and symposiums that focus on specific machine learning subfields, enabling you to delve deeper into your areas of interest.

3. Benefits of Attending:
Attending conferences and workshops offers several key benefits to beginners in machine learning. Firstly, it provides an opportunity to listen to leading experts in the field through keynote speeches and panel discussions. This exposure can enhance your understanding of the field's emerging concepts, challenges, and future directions. Additionally, these events often have tutorial sessions where domain experts offer in-depth explanations of fundamental concepts or advanced techniques. Leveraging these opportunities allows you to solidify your understanding and gain insights into practical applications.

4. Networking Opportunities:
Conferences and workshops present unparalleled networking opportunities, allowing you to interact with like-minded peers, potential mentors, researchers, and industry professionals. Networking can spark collaborations, help you find mentors, and even lead to job prospects. Approach each event with a proactive mindset, seek out individuals who share your research interests, and make an effort to connect with them during breaks, poster sessions, or social events. Remember, building relationships within the machine learning community is crucial for career growth and obtaining significant recommendations.

5. Presenting Research Work:
When attending conferences and workshops, strive to actively participate by either submitting research papers, presenting posters, or giving oral presentations. Presenting your work not only acts as a catalyst for discussions and receiving constructive feedback but also provides valuable exposure for your research, potentially attracting collaborators or employers. It is important to carefully follow the submission guidelines and deadlines for each event, ensuring that your work aligns with the specific theme or track.

6. Getting Involved as a Volunteer:
Volunteering at conferences and workshops can be a remarkable experience for beginners. Many events actively seek volunteers for various tasks like session management, organizing social

events, or managing social media. This unique opportunity allows you to experience the conference from a different perspective while creating connections with the organizing committee and presenters. Volunteering may also provide financial benefits, with some events offering waived registration fees or subsidized accommodations in exchange for your assistance.

7. Staying Informed and Engaged:
In addition to attending conferences and workshops, it is essential to stay informed and engaged with the machine learning community throughout the year. Explore popular online platforms such as arXiv, Medium, or Towards Data Science for recent research publications, articles, and insightful blogs on machine learning topics. Participating in online forums, such as Reddit's r/MachineLearning or LinkedIn groups, can facilitate discussions and knowledge sharing within the field. Regularly following influential researchers, organizations, and industry leaders on social media platforms like Twitter can further enhance your exposure to updates, news, and discussions in real-time.

In conclusion, participating in conferences and workshops is an excellent strategy for beginner machine learning enthusiasts. It facilitates learning from leading experts, discovering new research, networking with researchers and professionals, and presenting your own work to receive valuable feedback. Actively immersing yourself in these events and engaging with the broader machine learning community empowers growth, promotes collaboration, and supports long-term success in the field.

11.4 Cultivating a Lifelong Learning Mindset

In the ever-evolving field of machine learning, embracing a lifelong learning mindset is crucial for staying relevant and making continuous progress. As a beginner, it is essential to understand that acquiring a solid foundation in machine learning is just the beginning. The journey towards proficiency and mastery requires consistent effort and a mindset that welcomes continuous learning. Amidst this section, we will delve into the importance of cultivating a lifelong learning mindset in the context of machine learning and provide guidance on how to maintain this mindset throughout your career.

1. Embrace Curiosity:
One of the key qualities of a lifelong learner is a relentless curiosity about the world around them. Cultivate a curiosity that propels you to seek deeper insights, question existing approaches, and explore innovative solutions. Machine learning is a vast field that is rapidly expanding, making it even more essential to stay curious about emerging techniques, tools, and applications. Read research papers, attend conferences, and network with experts in the field to nurture a curiosity-driven approach to learning.

2. Emphasize Problem-Solving:
Machine learning is fundamentally centered around solving complex problems by leveraging data and algorithms. Developing a problem-solving mindset will be vital throughout your journey. Approach every problem as an opportunity to learn and improve your skills. Break down problems into manageable pieces, explore different approaches, and analyze critical insights gained from both successes and failures. By embracing a problem-solving mindset, you will build resilience

and continuously evolve your abilities.

3. Invest in Continuous Learning:
Machine learning algorithms, frameworks, and methodologies are continuously evolving. Embrace the fact that your learning should not halt after completing a course or mastering the basics. Allocate regular time for upskilling by engaging in learning activities such as online courses, tutorials, and books, or by participating in workshops or boot camps. Dedicate yourself to staying up to date with the latest developments to maintain a competitive edge in the field.

4. Foster Collaborative Learning:
Machine learning is a highly collaborative field encompassing diverse perspectives and expertise. Surround yourself with like-minded learners, join online forums or local communities, and engage in collaborative projects or competitions. By interacting with fellow learners and professionals, you can leverage their knowledge, learn from their experiences, and develop a robust network that contributes to your growth. Fostering collaborative learning will broaden your skill set and expose you to new ideas and challenges.

5. Embody Resilience:
Machine learning can be challenging at times, and setbacks are inevitable. Developing resilience is vital to overcome obstacles and persevere in your learning journey. Embrace failures as valuable learning experiences and use them as stepping stones towards improvement. Embodying resilience will allow you to navigate through difficulties, acknowledge your weaknesses, and embrace opportunities to grow both intellectually and professionally.

6. Stay Grounded:
With the rapid advancement of technology, it can be tempting to constantly seek the next flashy tool or technique. However, it is essential to remain grounded and focus on developing a profound understanding of fundamental concepts. Invest time in studying mathematics, statistics, and theoretical foundations of

machine learning to gain a holistic comprehension of the underlying principles. Building a strong theoretical foundation will enable you to adapt to new technologies and ensure a sustainable career in machine learning.

7. Seek feedback and self-reflection:
Regularly seek feedback from peers, mentors, or professionals in the field to gain valuable insights into your learning and development. Constructive criticism can highlight areas of improvement and help you fine-tune your learning strategy. Engage in self-reflection by consciously evaluating your strengths, weaknesses, and learning approaches. Identifying areas that need further improvement will guide your learning trajectory and foster continuous growth.

Cultivating a lifelong learning mindset is an ongoing process that requires dedication, passion, and the willingness to venture outside your comfort zone. Embrace the journey, stay adaptable, and continually challenge yourself to ensure progress in the dynamic field of machine learning. With dedication and resilience, you will discover countless opportunities for innovation and contribute to the advancements that shape the future of artificial intelligence and beyond.

Chapter 12: Future Trends in Machine Learning

Inside this final chapter, we will explore some of the future trends in machine learning and attempt to glimpse into the exciting possibilities and potential advancements on the horizon. While it is impossible to predict with absolute certainty what lies ahead, we can identify certain key areas that are primed for significant advancements within the field.

1. Deep Learning and Neural Networks:
Deep learning has already proven to be a game-changer in various domains, such as computer vision, natural language processing, and speech recognition. In the future, we can expect further advancements in neural networks, including the development of more efficient architectures, the ability to process multimodal data, and the incorporation of progressive learning techniques to continually improve models.

2. Explaining AI:
One of the major challenges currently faced by machine learning is the lack of transparency and interpretability in AI models. As machine learning algorithms are integrated into critical systems, there is a growing need to understand the decisions made by these models. Future research will focus on developing methodologies and techniques to explain how and why models arrive at their predictions, fostering better trust and accountability in AI systems.

3. Transfer Learning and Few-Shot Learning:
Transfer learning has already provided a breakthrough in training models on one task and applying them to related tasks with less supervision. However, currently, this transfer is mostly limited to similar domains or tasks. Future research will delve

into leveraging transfer learning across increasingly diverse domains, allowing models to learn from a broader spectrum of data and generalize better. Additionally, few-shot learning aims to enable models to learn from only a few examples, pushing the boundaries of what is currently possible with limited labeled data.

4. Privacy and Ethics:
As machine learning becomes increasingly intertwined with our daily lives, there is a growing concern for the privacy and ethical implications of AI. Research is being conducted to develop privacy-preserving machine learning techniques that allow models to learn from sensitive data without compromising individuals' privacy. Ethical considerations are also being addressed by focusing on topics such as bias and fairness, highlighting the need for responsible and unbiased AI algorithms.

5. Edge Computing and IoT:
The proliferation of IoT devices has resulted in an incredibly large and distributed amount of data generated at the edge of the network. Machine learning on edge devices brings several benefits, including reduced latency, enhanced privacy, and decreased bandwidth requirements. Future trends will aim to push the boundaries of what can be achieved on resource-constrained devices, integrating machine learning capabilities closer to the data source.

6. Robotics and Reinforcement Learning:
Advancements in robotics and reinforcement learning are shaping the future of intelligent automation. Reinforcement learning, in particular, offers the promise of endowing machines with the ability to learn complex tasks through interacting with their environment and receiving rewards or penalties. As reinforcement learning techniques improve, we can anticipate robotics becoming more capable, leading to a wide range of applications, such as autonomous vehicles, smart manufacturing, and domestic robotics.

7. Collaborative Machine Learning:
Traditionally, machine learning has relied on centralizing vast amounts of data in a single location for training models. Collaborative machine learning seeks to address privacy concerns by allowing models to be trained across multiple distributed entities without sharing the raw data. Federated learning, for example, enables devices to locally learn from their data and then aggregate their knowledge to improve the shared model, providing a more privacy-preserving approach to machine learning.

While these trends represent just a glimpse into the vast landscape of future possibilities in machine learning, they highlight the tremendous potential for growth and innovation within the field. By staying informed, embracing new methodologies, and being adaptable, you will be well-prepared to contribute to and shape the future of machine learning. Exciting times lie ahead, and as we strive towards advancements and breakthroughs, always remember that the quest to explore the unknown is integral to the ethos of machine learning.

12.1 Exploring Emerging Technologies in ML

12.1 Exploring Emerging Technologies in Machine Learning

In recent years, machine learning has revolutionized various industries, leading to groundbreaking advancements in technology. As a beginner in the field, it is essential to understand the vast array of emerging technologies in machine learning that hold immense promise for the future. Amidst the details of this section, we will delve into some of these exciting innovations, showcasing their potential and pondering their implications.

1. Deep Learning: Deep learning has gained significant attention due to its remarkable ability to learn and recognize patterns from vast amounts of data. Inspired by the architecture of the human brain, neural networks underpin deep learning models. They consist of interconnected layers of artificial neurons capable of hierarchical data representation and abstraction. Deep learning has proved immensely successful in various domains, such as computer vision, natural language processing, and even game-playing agents.

2. Reinforcement Learning: Reinforcement learning tackles the challenge of teaching an agent to make optimal decisions in a given environment. It operates on the basis of reward-based learning, wherein an agent learns by interacting with its surroundings and receiving feedback in the form of rewards or punishments. Reinforcement learning has shown tremendous potential in domains like robotics, autonomous driving, and game optimization, manifesting the ability to uncover complex strategies and achieve superhuman performance.

3. Generative Models: Generative models allow machines to generate novel and synthetic data that closely resembles real-world observations. Two popular types of generative models are Variational Autoencoders (VAEs) and Generative Adversarial Networks (GANs). VAEs aim to learn the underlying distribution of the input data and generate new instances from it. On the other hand, GANs consist of a generator and a discriminator engaged in an adversarial game, whereby the generator tries to generate realistic data while the discriminator attempts to distinguish between real and synthetic data. Such generative models find extensive use in tasks like image synthesis, text generation, and data augmentation.

4. Transfer Learning: Transfer learning leverages knowledge gained from solving one problem and applies it to a different, but related, problem. Instead of training a machine learning model from scratch, transfer learning facilitates the reuse of pre-trained models that have learned general features from tasks with abundant labeled data. This approach saves valuable time and resources, making it especially useful when dealing with limited datasets. The application of transfer learning extends across multiple domains, including computer vision, natural language processing, and audio processing.

5. Edge Computing in ML: Edge computing brings the computational power and intelligence of machine learning closer to the data source, reducing communication latency and network bandwidth requirements. This eliminates the need to always rely on cloud infrastructure for running machine learning models. Edge computing in machine learning has prominent benefits where real-time decision-making or sensitive data handling is crucial. Applications like smart homes, autonomous vehicles, and IoT devices greatly benefit from the edge's low latency and real-time processing capabilities.

6. Explainable AI: The influence and adoption of machine learning models grow at an unprecedented rate. However, there is an emerging need to understand and interpret their predictions and decisions. Explainable AI aims to shed light on

the reasoning and decision-making process of machine learning models, ensuring transparency and accountability. Techniques like contextual importance, saliency maps, and rule extraction empower individuals to trust and navigate through models' outputs responsibly.

7. Quantum Machine Learning: Quantum computing holds the promise of providing exponential computational capabilities compared to classical computers. The intersection of quantum computing and machine learning, known as quantum machine learning, explores the synergy between these two domains. Harnessing quantum principles, researchers are working towards developing machine learning algorithms that can utilize quantum computers' superior processing power.

With these emerging technologies, machine learning continues to push boundaries and open new avenues for exploration. As a beginner, it is crucial to stay curious, up-to-date, and embrace the opportunities these technologies bring forth. Remember, machine learning is a rapidly evolving field, and being aware of emerging trends will play a pivotal role in your journey towards becoming a proficient machine learning practitioner.

12.2 The Role of Explainable AI and Model Interpretability

In recent years, there has been a growing interest in harnessing the power of artificial intelligence (AI) and machine learning algorithms to improve decision-making processes across various domains. However, as these models become more complex and capable of processing massive amounts of data, understanding how and why they arrive at their predictions becomes increasingly difficult. This is where Explainable AI or XAI and model interpretability play a crucial role.

Explainable AI refers to the ability of machine learning algorithms to explain their decision-making process in a way that humans can understand. This goes beyond just providing the final prediction or result; it involves providing the rationale behind it. Model interpretability, on the other hand, focuses on understanding how the inner workings of a machine learning model contribute to its output.

The need for explainability and interpretability arises due to several reasons. First and foremost, AI models can have serious real-world consequences. For instance, if a machine learning model is used to determine creditworthiness, denying someone a loan based on an opaque algorithm could have unfair and biased implications. Similarly, in healthcare, it is crucial to understand why a given model predicts a certain disease before making critical decisions.

Explainable AI and model interpretability enable the detection and mitigation of biases that may be inherent in the data or the algorithms themselves. By opening up the black box of complex machine learning models, it becomes easier to identify any discriminatory patterns and enhance fairness and transparency in decision-making processes. This has ethical, legal, and social implications that are vital in today's AI-driven world.

Moreover, explainability also increases trust and adoption of AI systems. When AI models provide understandable explanations for their predictions, users and stakeholders are more likely to trust and embrace the technology. This is particularly relevant in regulated industries, such as finance and healthcare, where justifications for decisions are required.

There are several techniques and approaches to achieving explainability and interpretability in AI models. Let's explore a few of them:

1. Rule-based models: Using predefined rules to make predictions provides transparency, as the model's decision-making process can be explicitly explained based on these rules. However, rule-based models might lack the flexibility to capture complex relationships within the data.

2. Feature importance: Identifying the input features that contribute the most to a model's prediction can help in understanding its decision-making process. Techniques like permutation importance, SHapley Additive exPlanations (SHAP), and partial dependence plots (PDPs) can shed light on feature-level influence.

3. Local interpretability: Instead of trying to interpret the entire model, a local interpretability approach focuses on understanding specific instances where a decision is taken. Techniques like LIME (Local Interpretable Model-Agnostic Explanations) and SHAP-LIME hybrid methods highlight the importance of individual instances in the decision-making process.

4. Prototypes and rule extraction: Creating simplified prototypes or instances representing the majority behavior of a model can offer insights into its decision process. Decision trees can often be a useful tool for extracting simplified rules from complex

models.

5. Visualizations: By visualizing the intermediate processes and final predictions of a model, it becomes easier to grasp its decision-making mechanism. Techniques like saliency maps, activation maximization, heatmaps, and attention mechanisms help in visualizing neural network-based models.

6. Simpler model explanations: Building simpler, interpretable models that approximate the complex model's behavior, known as surrogate models, can provide a comprehensible understanding of the high performing model. These surrogate models act as proxies for the black-box models and help replicate the predictions in a more explainable manner.

It's important to note that not all machine learning models are equally amenable to explainability and interpretability. Deep neural networks, for example, are often considered black boxes due to their intricate architectures and internal hierarchies. However, researchers and practitioners are actively exploring methods to make even complex models more interpretable.

In conclusion, explainable AI and model interpretability are becoming increasingly important in the field of machine learning. They play a pivotal role in addressing the ethical and social implications of AI systems, enhancing transparency and fairness, and fostering trust and adoption. By employing various techniques like rule-based models, feature importance analysis, local interpretability, and visualizations, it becomes possible to demystify the black box nature of complex machine learning models. With ongoing research and development in this area, the future holds great promise for making AI more explainable and interpretable for users and stakeholders alike.

12.3 Integration of AI in Industry 4.0

In recent years, there has been a significant buzz surrounding Industry 4.0, also known as the fourth industrial revolution. This revolution is driven by the integration of various technologies, and artificial intelligence (AI) is among the most promising ones. The applications of AI in Industry 4.0 hold immense potential to transform the way industries operate and produce goods and services.

Integration of AI in Industry 4.0 is driven by several factors, including advancements in machine learning algorithms, computing power, and data availability. Engulfed by this section, we will delve into the details of how AI is being integrated into different aspects of Industry 4.0, providing you with a comprehensive understanding of its applications and benefits.

12.3.1 Predictive Maintenance:

One of the areas where AI has revolutionized industrial processes is predictive maintenance. Traditionally, industries perform routine maintenance tasks on machinery and equipment at predetermined time intervals. However, this approach often results in unnecessary downtime and maintenance costs.

With the integration of AI in Industry 4.0, machines can now be equipped with sensors and AI algorithms that continuously monitor their performance. These algorithms analyze real-time data collected by sensors to identify patterns and potential faults. As a result, maintenance tasks can be planned only when needed, optimizing productivity and cost-effectiveness.

12.3.2 Quality Control:

Achieving high-quality standards in manufacturing processes is crucial for industries. AI has emerged as a game-changer in quality control within Industry 4.0. Machine learning models can be trained with vast amounts of historical data to recognize patterns associated with good or defective products.

By analyzing real-time data from production lines, AI algorithms can detect anomalies and quickly identify any deviations from the standard production process. This enables early intervention, preventing defective products from reaching customers and minimizing losses. Moreover, AI-powered quality control systems continuously learn from feedback, improving their accuracy over time.

12.3.3 Supply Chain Optimization:

Efficient supply chain management is fundamental for maintaining competitive advantage in the fast-paced world of Industry 4.0. AI algorithms are increasingly being used to optimize supply chain processes, addressing challenges such as demand forecasting, inventory management, and logistics optimization.

Through AI-powered predictive analytics, demand forecasting becomes more accurate, helping industries reduce the risk of overstock or stockouts. AI algorithms can also optimize inventory management by considering multiple factors like market trends, supplier performance, and production capabilities. Furthermore, AI can optimize logistics routes through real-time analysis of transportation data, reducing lead times and transportation costs.

12.3.4 Human-Robot Collaboration:

Another area where AI integration in Industry 4.0 is making strides is human-robot collaboration. Collaborative robots, also known as cobots, are equipped with AI algorithms that enable them to work safely alongside human operators.

Traditional industrial robots require programming to follow predefined tasks in a controlled environment. However, with the integration of AI, cobots can adapt to dynamic environments, learn from human interactions, and make real-time decisions. This opens up new possibilities for industries, facilitating flexible and efficient production processes while ensuring the safety of human workers.

12.3.5 Product Personalization and Customization:

In the era of Industry 4.0, customers increasingly demand personalized and customized products. AI algorithms play a crucial role in fulfilling these requirements. By analyzing customer data, machine learning models can gather insights into individual preferences and tailor manufacturing processes accordingly.

From personalized product design to customized manufacturing, AI helps industries meet customers' unique demands. This integration allows for efficient production flows without sacrificing product quality and diversity.

12.3.6 Energy Management:

Sustainable practices are becoming a priority for industries seeking to reduce their environmental footprint. AI in Industry 4.0 can significantly contribute to energy management and conservation efforts.

By analyzing real-time energy consumption data, AI algorithms can identify energy inefficiencies and optimize energy usage. Machine learning models can predict energy demand patterns, enabling proactive load balancing, demand response, and overall energy savings.

In Conclusion:

The integration of AI in Industry 4.0 is revolutionizing industrial operations across various domains. From predictive maintenance and quality control to supply chain optimization and human-robot collaboration, AI technologies are transforming industries, making them more efficient, cost-effective, and sustainable.

As beginners in the field of machine learning, exploring the practical applications of AI in Industry 4.0 offers valuable insights into the potential of this transformative technology. Harnessing the power of AI allows industries to stay ahead of the curve, offering enhanced product customization, improved resource management, and increased productivity. Embracing AI integration in Industry 4.0 paves the way for a future where industries thrive on intelligent systems, paving the path towards a more prosperous and digitally connected world.

12.4 Preparing for the Future: Key Considerations

As we dive deeper into the world of machine learning, it is essential to recognize the importance of preparing for the future. Machine learning is a rapidly evolving field, and being proactive in considering key aspects can greatly contribute to your success as a practitioner. Within the confines of this section, we will explore some pivotal considerations to help you prepare for the future of machine learning.

1. Stay Updated with the Latest Developments:
Machine learning is characterized by constant advancements and breakthroughs. To stay ahead, it is crucial to dedicate time to continuous learning. Read research papers, subscribe to machine learning blogs, and follow reputed experts on social media channels to stay informed about the latest developments. Furthermore, participating in machine learning competitions can also expose you to cutting-edge techniques and algorithms.

2. Enhance Your Knowledge in Related Domains:
Machine learning is often applied to solve complex problems in various domains such as healthcare, finance, and manufacturing. To excel in applying machine learning effectively in these fields, it is essential to have domain knowledge. Spend time understanding the nuances and principles of the specific domain you are interested in, as it will help you tailor machine learning algorithms to suit the unique circumstances within that domain.

3. Focus on Ethical Decision-making:
As machine learning becomes more pervasive, it is crucial to consider the ethical implications of your work. Machine learning models have the potential to reinforce biases and perpetuate discrimination. By being aware of these issues and addressing

them proactively, you can positively contribute to the field. Develop an understanding of fairness, accountability, transparency, and ethics while designing and training machine learning models. Be mindful of the potential impacts of your work on society as a whole.

4. Prioritize Data Privacy and Security:
With the increasing availability and utilization of massive datasets, ensuring data privacy and security has become paramount. As a machine learning practitioner, you must be knowledgeable about data protection laws and regulations in your jurisdiction. Avoid using sensitive data unless necessary, and implement stringent security measures to safeguard the data you handle. Considering privacy and security during model development will secure your work and build trust with stakeholders.

5. Embrace Continual Improvement:
Machine learning models, even after deployment, require proactive maintenance and improvement. It is essential to create robust monitoring processes to identify and address issues promptly. Continuously collect feedback from end-users and stakeholders, and integrate their insights into your models. As new sources of data become available, explore their potential for further accuracy and analyze how they align with existing models. By continuously refining and fine-tuning your models, you can ensure their efficiency and effectiveness over time.

6. Collaboration and Interdisciplinary Training:
Machine learning is not a solitary endeavor. Collaborative approaches bring together diverse skill sets and perspectives, leading to innovative breakthroughs. Engage with the wider machine learning community by attending conferences, participating in workshops, and joining online forums. Collaboration allows for the exchange of ideas, exposing you to different approaches and challenges.

7. Develop Communication and Visualization Skills:
The ability to effectively communicate machine learning

concepts is a valuable skill, both within the machine learning community and when dealing with non-technical stakeholders. Develop your communication skills to explain complex algorithms and concepts in simple terms. Visualization is an influential tool for communicating insights obtained from machine learning models. Invest time in learning visualization techniques to convey results and findings more effectively.

8. Embrace Open-source Practices:
Machine learning would not be where it is today without the rich ecosystem of open-source tools and libraries available. Embrace open-source practices and contribute to the community by sharing your code, creating tutorials and examples, and reporting bugs. By actively participating in open-source projects, you enhance your visibility, learn from experienced practitioners, and collaborate with like-minded individuals.

As you venture into the exciting universe of machine learning, keep in mind that preparing for the future is key to succeeding in this dynamic field. Stay informed about cutting-edge technologies, consider ethical implications, prioritize data privacy and security, and adopt a mindset of continual improvement. Through collaboration, effective communication, and embracing open-source practices, you can make meaningful contributions to the machine learning community while preparing yourself for the future of this transformative technology.

Chapter 13: Realworld Applications and Case Studies

Real-world Applications and Case Studies
Within these chapter, we dive into the practical side of machine learning and explore various real-world applications where machine learning techniques are being extensively used. Understanding these applications will help you grasp the immense potential of machine learning in solving complex problems and making data-driven predictions in a wide range of domains. Additionally, we will examine some compelling case studies that highlight the achievements and impact of this technology across different industries.

1. Natural Language Processing:
Natural Language Processing (NLP) is a fascinating field within machine learning that focuses on enabling computers to understand and generate human language. We discuss various applications of NLP, such as machine translation, sentiment analysis, question-answering systems, and chatbots. We delve into the underlying techniques, such as word embeddings, recurrent neural networks, and transformers, that power these applications and enable computers to truly understand language.

2. Computer Vision:
Computer Vision is another exciting area where machine learning has made significant advancements. We explore applications like object detection, image classification, semantic segmentation, and facial recognition. We explain the fundamental concepts of Convolutional Neural Networks (CNNs) and their role in analyzing visual data. Understanding computer vision applications will help you grasp how machine learning algorithms can interpret and extract meaningful information from images and videos.

3. Recommender Systems:
Recommender systems play a crucial role in various domains, including e-commerce and entertainment. We discuss collaborative filtering techniques and content-based approaches used in recommender systems. We analyze how machine learning algorithms make personalized recommendations based on user preferences and item features. We examine case studies of popular recommender systems like those implemented by Netflix and Amazon to understand how machine learning is driving personalization and enhancing the user experience.

4. Healthcare and Medicine:
Machine learning has tremendous potential to revolutionize healthcare and medicine. We explore applications such as disease diagnosis, treatment recommendation, and drug discovery. We delve into how advanced machine learning techniques like deep learning and reinforcement learning are being used to analyze medical images, such as X-rays and MRIs, identify potential disease patterns, and create predictive models for patient outcomes.

5. Finance and Stock Market:
The finance industry has greatly benefited from machine learning applications. We discuss how algorithms are used for credit scoring, fraud detection, investment analysis, and stock market prediction. We explore the techniques that help identify market trends and make predictions with regression, time series analysis, and ensemble models. We cover compelling case studies that highlight the impact of machine learning on the financial sector.

6. Autonomous Vehicles:
Autonomous vehicles are an epitome of advanced machine learning applications. We explore the concepts and algorithms behind self-driving cars, including perception systems, decision-making processes, and control mechanisms. We discuss real-time sensor data processing, object detection and tracking, and the critical role of varied machine learning techniques in

enabling safe and efficient autonomous transportation.

Conclusion:
Real-world applications highlight the infinite opportunities and benefits that machine learning brings across diverse domains. Having explored the realms of natural language processing, computer vision, recommender systems, healthcare, finance, and autonomous vehicles, you have gained an insight into the vast potential of machine learning in transforming our lives. Armed with this knowledge, you are now better equipped to dive into more complex machine learning problems and explore additional domains where this evolving field holds the power to unlock innovative solutions.

13.1 Applications Across Industries: Healthcare, Finance, and more

Machine learning has rapidly revolutionized various industries by automating processes, extracting insights from vast amounts of data, and enabling predictions that were once seemingly impossible. This chapter delves into some prominent applications of machine learning across industries, with a strong focus on healthcare and finance.

13.1.1 Healthcare

In the healthcare sector, machine learning is transforming patient care, diagnosis, treatment plans, and drug discovery. One significant application is in medical imaging analysis. Machine learning algorithms can learn to identify patterns in medical images, enabling accurate diagnoses and faster treatment decisions. For example, in the field of radiology, algorithms can aid in detecting anomalies such as tumors, enabling early intervention and potentially saving lives.

Additionally, machine learning contributes to personalized medicine by analyzing an individual's genetic and clinical data to determine personalized treatment plans. This technique holds substantial promise for accurate and targeted therapies, avoiding unnecessary side effects, and minimizing treatment cost.

Another significant application lies in disease prediction and outbreak prevention. By analyzing vast amounts of historical and real-time data, machine learning models can forecast disease spread, identify vulnerable populations, and optimize resource allocation. Such insights are instrumental in proactively managing public health crises and saving lives on a larger scale.

13.1.2 Finance

In the finance industry, machine learning algorithms have enabled advanced data analysis, risk assessment, fraud detection, and portfolio management. Banks and financial institutions extensively use these techniques for activities such as credit scoring, customer segmentation, and recommender systems.

One of the essential applications in finance is algorithmic trading. Machine learning models analyze historical data, identify patterns, and make informed predictions about market trends. Traders can leverage these predictions to make faster and more accurate investment decisions, resulting in improved profitability.

Moreover, machine learning is used extensively in fraud detection and prevention. Algorithms can learn from patterns and anomalies in financial transactions to identify suspicious behavior, preventing fraudulent activities like identity theft or unauthorized access to accounts. These algorithms continuously adapt and stay alert to new forms of fraud, contributing to enhanced security measures.

Another emerging application of machine learning in finance is in the field of personal finance management and automated financial advisors. These systems can analyze an individual's financial data, predict spending patterns, and provide recommendations on saving strategies, investment opportunities, and debt management.

13.1.3 Other Industries

Beyond healthcare and finance, machine learning finds applications in numerous other industries. In retail, machine learning is leveraged for demand forecasting, inventory management, price optimization, and personalized product recommendations based on a customer's browsing and purchasing history.

The transportation industry uses machine learning techniques for route optimization, vehicle maintenance prediction, and autonomous vehicle development. These technologies are revolutionizing transportation safety, reducing operational costs, and improving overall efficiency.

In the manufacturing sector, machine learning facilitates predictive maintenance, quality control, and process optimization. By analyzing sensor data from machinery, models can predict failures, schedule maintenance before breakdowns occur, and ensure smooth production cycles.

In conclusion, machine learning holds great potential in transforming various industries. From healthcare to finance, and even retail, transportation, and manufacturing – countless applications have emerged, improving efficiency, providing valuable insights, and revolutionizing traditional practices. As innovation in the field of machine learning advances, more industries will undoubtedly embrace this technology to unlock new opportunities and overcome complex challenges.

13.2 Success Stories and Case Studies

In the world of machine learning, success stories and case studies play a crucial role in showcasing the potential and application of this powerful technology. By examining real-world examples, beginners can gain valuable insights into how machine learning algorithms have been used to tackle complex problems and achieve remarkable achievements. Surrounded by this section, we will explore some captivating success stories and case studies that exemplify the transformative impact of machine learning.

1. Autonomous Vehicles - Transformation of Transportation:
One of the most captivating success stories in recent years has been the development of autonomous vehicles. Companies like Tesla and Waymo have leveraged machine learning algorithms to create vehicles that can navigate and drive independently. Through the use of sensor data fusion, computer vision, and reinforcement learning techniques, these vehicles are capable of assessing the environment, making split-second decisions, and ensuring passenger safety. Case studies in this field delve into the challenges faced during development, advancements in deep learning models for real-time decision-making, and the ethical implications associated with autonomous vehicles.

2. Healthcare - Revolutionizing Diagnostics:
Another remarkable area where machine learning has demonstrated enormous potential is in healthcare. Case studies in this field focus on the use of machine learning algorithms to predict diseases, improve diagnoses, and streamline treatment plans. For instance, researchers have leveraged deep learning models to analyze medical images and accurately detect diseases like cancer or diabetic retinopathy. Additionally, machine learning has been applied in genomics to analyze vast amounts of genetic data, aiding in the identification of potential genetic

markers linked to diseases.

3. Natural Language Processing - Conversational AI:
Conversational AI has come a long way, thanks to advancements in natural language processing (NLP) enabled by machine learning algorithms. Case studies in this domain demonstrate the power of NLP models to understand and generate human-like text. Examples include chatbots and virtual assistants like Siri and Alexa, which leverage machine learning algorithms to provide personalized assistance, understand user intents, and generate coherent responses. Case studies delve into the training process of these language models, the challenges of generating contextually appropriate responses, and the potential future directions of NLP research.

4. Fraud Detection - Enhancing Security:
Machine learning has made significant strides in fraud detection by leveraging powerful algorithms to identify patterns and anomalies in vast amounts of data. Case studies in this field explore how machine learning techniques have been used to detect fraudulent financial transactions, network intrusions, or even identify fake reviews online. By analyzing historical data, machine learning models can develop predictive capabilities to identify suspicious behavior or outliers, allowing early detection and prevention of fraudulent activities.

5. Entertainment - Personalized Recommendations:
Companies like Netflix and Spotify have harnessed the power of machine learning to provide personalized recommendations that enhance user experience and engagement. Case studies here emphasize the use of collaborative filtering techniques, content-based filtering, and embedding models to understand user preferences and provide relevant suggestions. Exploring the algorithms and strategies employed can give beginners insights into how to design recommendation systems that cater to individual user tastes and preferences.

Incorporating success stories and case studies enables beginners to see the practical applications of machine learning, fostering a deeper understanding of its benefits and possibilities. Through these examples, learners can gain inspiration, learn best practices, and explore the fascinating technological advancements fueled by machine learning algorithms.

Remember, success stories are not only intended to showcase triumphs but also to shed light on the challenges faced, the ethics involved, and the potential limitations. By learning from both successful and unsuccessful case studies, beginners can gain a more holistic understanding of the complexities and potential pitfalls of implementing machine learning solutions in various domains.

13.3 Challenges Faced in Realworld Deployments

13.3 Challenges Faced in Real-world Deployments

As machine learning algorithms continue to advance and gain popularity, there is an increasing focus on deploying these algorithms in real-world scenarios. However, the deployment process comes with its fair share of challenges. Amidst this chapter, we will explore some of the main challenges faced in real-world deployments of machine learning models and discuss potential solutions.

1. Data quality and availability:
One of the foremost challenges in deploying machine learning models is the availability of high-quality data. Real-world data often contains noise, missing values, outliers, and other inconsistencies, which can affect the accuracy and reliability of the trained models. Furthermore, obtaining relevant and sufficient data can also be a significant challenge. It is crucial to invest effort in data collection and preprocessing to ensure the deployment of robust and accurate models.

2. Model interpretability:
While complex machine learning algorithms such as neural networks often provide powerful results, their outputs are often considered black boxes. Understanding and interpreting the decisions made by these models can be challenging, especially in sensitive domains where accountability and transparency are crucial. Addressing this challenge requires exploring techniques that provide insights into model predictions and ensuring that models are explainable and understandable by humans.

3. Scaling and performance:

Deploying machine learning models that can handle large-scale data and maintain acceptable performance levels can be challenging. Real-world applications often experience an ever-growing volume of data, requiring models to scale effectively. Furthermore, as models become more complex, their inference times may increase, resulting in decreased efficiency. Overcoming these challenges involves implementing efficient algorithms, optimizing hardware resources, and considering distributed computing solutions.

4. Continuous learning and updating:
In many real-world scenarios, the data distribution can change over time. Models that are not updated may become outdated and lose their accuracy. Deploying machine learning models that can adapt and continuously learn from new data is crucial. This involves designing systems that incorporate feedback loops, monitoring performance, and retraining models periodically or dynamically as new data becomes available.

5. Ethical and legal considerations:
Deploying machine learning models in real-world applications requires careful attention to ethical and legal considerations. Models can inadvertently perpetuate biases, discriminate, or invade privacy. It is essential to ensure fairness, transparency, and compliance with relevant policies and regulations. Addressing these challenges involves creating frameworks for responsible and ethical deployment, conducting thorough audits, and providing oversight mechanisms.

6. Handling uncertainty:
Real-world deployments often have to deal with various sources of uncertainty such as noisy data, changing environments, and partial observations. Uncertainty can significantly affect the reliability and robustness of machine learning models. Addressing this challenge involves incorporating uncertainty estimation techniques such as probabilistic models, Bayesian methods, or ensemble approaches, which enable quantifying and managing uncertainty in predictions.

7. Limited resources and deployment constraints:
In real-world scenarios, there can be limitations in the availability of computational resources, power, memory, or network bandwidth. These constraints can impact the selection, deployment, and adaptation of machine learning models. Adapting models to limited resources often requires trade-offs, including model simplification, feature selection, or using more efficient algorithms. It is crucial to carefully consider these constraints during the design and implementation stages.

8. Integration with existing systems:
Integrating machine learning models into existing infrastructure or systems can be complex and challenging. Coordinating with different domains, dealing with legacy systems or proprietary formats, and ensuring interoperability are common hurdles. Seamless integration necessitates designing well-defined interfaces, adopting open standards, and aligning model outputs with the requirements of the downstream systems.

These are just some of the challenges that arise when deploying machine learning models in real-world scenarios. It is important to acknowledge and address these challenges to ensure the successful implementation and long-term viability of machine learning solutions. Follow the best practices outlined in this book, continuously stay updated with advancements in the field, and engage with the machine learning community to overcome these challenges effectively.

13.4 Inspiring Examples of Machine Learning Impact

Machine learning has rapidly gained prominence across various domains and is revolutionizing industries worldwide. Inside this chapter, we will delve into some inspiring examples of how machine learning has created a significant impact in different sectors, emphasizing its potential and versatility.

1. Healthcare:
One of the most promising areas where machine learning has made evident strides is in healthcare. From disease diagnosis to personalized treatment plans, machine learning algorithms have enhanced the accuracy and efficacy of medical procedures. For instance, AI-powered algorithms have revolutionized radiology by identifying anomalies in medical imaging, allowing for faster and more accurate diagnosis.

2. Transportation:
Machine learning has also brought immense advancement to transportation systems. Self-driving cars are an exemplary manifestation of machine learning impact. Using complex algorithms, these vehicles analyze real-time data from sensors and cameras to navigate highways and urban streets safely. This technology not only improves road safety but also offers potential opportunities for enhancing fuel efficiency.

3. Finance:
The finance industry has extensively benefitted from machine learning applications. Trading algorithms use complex models to predict market trends, aiding investors in making informed decisions. Fraud detection systems utilize machine learning to detect patterns and anomalies, preventing monetary losses for individuals and organizations. Moreover, loan approval

processes have become more efficient and accurate through machine learning algorithms analyzing user profiles and credit history.

4. Retail:
Machine learning has transformed retail by enabling personalized shopping experiences. Recommender systems built upon machine learning algorithms analyze consumer behavior to recommend products matched to individual preferences. This not only improves customer satisfaction but also enables businesses to leverage market trends and achieve higher conversion rates.

5. Manufacturing:
Machine learning algorithms have made manufacturing more efficient and cost-effective by optimizing production processes. AI systems monitor real-time sensor data to identify potential machine failures or quality defects, enabling proactive maintenance. This leads to reduced downtime, improved productivity, and enhanced product quality.

6. Agriculture:
Modern agriculture has also embraced machine learning techniques to optimize crop production. Satellite imagery, weather data, and soil analysis are combined using machine learning algorithms to derive insights on crop health, pest identification, and the optimal usage of resources like water and fertilizers. Such practices help farmers maximize yield while reducing environmental impact.

7. Natural Language Processing:
Machine learning algorithms have made remarkable advances in natural language processing (NLP). Virtual assistants like Amazon's Alexa or Apple's Siri leverage machine learning to understand voice commands, enabling users to interact with technology more effortlessly. Machine translation systems have also seen significant improvements, enabling efficient communication across languages.

8. Energy:
Machine learning facilitates the development of smart energy solutions, enabling the efficient distribution and consumption of power. Energy management systems analyze massive data sets to optimize energy supply and demand, enhancing grid stability and reducing waste. Machine learning algorithms optimize renewable energy generation, making it more predictable and reducing reliance on traditional fossil fuels.

9. Entertainment:
Machine learning has transformed the entertainment industry by offering tailored content and personalized recommendations. Streaming platforms like Netflix use sophisticated algorithms to analyze users' viewing habits and preferences, suggesting movies and shows that individuals are more likely to enjoy. This has revolutionized the way we consume entertainment.

10. Environmental Preservation:
Machine learning is also contributing to environmental preservation efforts. Endangered species conservation benefits from algorithms that analyze patterns in wildlife behavior and habitat. Machine learning assists in monitoring, predicting, and mitigating environmental threats, ultimately aiding in the preservation of biodiversity.

These inspiring examples represent just a fraction of the immense impact machine learning has had on various fields. The versatility and potential of this technology continue to unfold, offering endless possibilities for innovation and advancement. As you embark on your machine learning journey, be prepared to explore and contribute to this remarkable revolution that is shaping the world around us.

Chapter 14: Challenges and Limitations in ML

Challenges and Limitations in Machine Learning
As exciting and promising as machine learning (ML) may be, it is essential to acknowledge that this field is not without its fair share of challenges and limitations. Inside this chapter, we will explore and discuss several key challenges that are commonly encountered when working with ML algorithms. Understanding these limitations will help beginners navigate the field of machine learning more effectively while providing a more realistic perspective on its capabilities.

1. Data Quality and Availability:
One of the fundamental challenges in ML is ensuring the quality and availability of data. ML algorithms heavily rely on vast amounts of high-quality data to function optimally. However, obtaining such data can be a daunting task. Issues like missing values, inconsistent formatting, and biased datasets can significantly impact the effectiveness and fairness of ML models. Furthermore, in certain domains, accessing large and representative datasets can be difficult due to privacy concerns and legal constraints.

2. Overfitting and Underfitting:
Ensuring a ML model generalizes well to unseen data is essential. Overfitting occurs when a model learns the training data too well, resulting in reduced performance on new data. This happens when a model becomes too complex or when there is limited training data available for effective learning. On the other hand, underfitting occurs when a model is too simplistic to capture the underlying patterns in the data. Balancing these two extremes is a critical challenge in machine learning.

3. Feature Engineering:
Feature engineering involves selecting and transforming the relevant input features for training an ML model. While ML algorithms have the ability to discover complex patterns, they heavily rely on the quality and relevance of the features provided. Identifying the right set of features often requires domain expertise and can significantly influence the performance of the model. Finding meaningful feature representations is a challenge in itself, demanding thorough exploration and iteration.

4. Interpretability and Explainability:
One of the limitations of many ML models is their lack of interpretability. Complex models like deep neural networks often behave like black boxes, making it challenging to understand how they arrive at their predictions. This is especially problematic in domains where model interpretability is crucial, such as healthcare or finance. Addressing this challenge is an active area of research, focusing on developing techniques that can explain the reasoning behind ML predictions.

5. Bias and Fairness:
ML models can inadvertently incorporate bias present in the training data, perpetuating existing societal bias or discriminating against certain groups. Bias in ML can manifest in many forms, including gender bias, racial bias, and class bias. Ensuring fairness in ML models is a crucial challenge that requires careful attention throughout the entire development lifecycle. Techniques like data augmentation, preprocessing algorithms, and regularized learning are actively researched to overcome this limitation.

6. Scalability and Performance:
While many ML algorithms perform exceptionally well on small or moderate-sized datasets, their scalability to larger datasets or real-time applications can present significant challenges. Training complex models with vast amounts of data can require substantial computational resources and time, limiting the model's feasibility in certain scenarios. Balancing scalability with

performance efficiently is critical, and ongoing research focuses on developing hardware accelerators and distributed learning techniques for large-scale ML systems.

7. Adversarial Attacks:
Adversarial attacks come into play when malicious actors intentionally manipulate the input data to deceive ML models. These attacks exploit vulnerabilities in the model's decision-making process, potentially leading to severe consequences. Resistant to such attacks is a challenging task, as models must be designed to handle and detect adversarial examples effectively. Robust ML models that can withstand such attacks are an active research area.

Conclusion:
Although machine learning has rapidly advanced in recent years, it is important to recognize the inherent challenges and limitations associated with the field. Addressing these challenges requires a combination of technical skills, domain knowledge, and in-depth understanding of the algorithms. As you continue your journey in machine learning, staying aware of these challenges will allow you to build more robust and reliable models, moving closer to unlocking the full potential of this exciting field.

14.1 Recognizing Common Challenges in ML

14.1 Recognizing Common Challenges in Machine Learning

Machine Learning (ML) has gained immense popularity in recent years and is revolutionizing industries by enabling computers to learn from data and make intelligent decisions. However, despite its potential, implementing ML algorithms and models can be challenging, especially for beginners. Amidst the details of this section, we will explore some common challenges that learners might encounter during their journey into the world of machine learning.

1. Data Preprocessing:
One of the initial hurdles in ML revolves around preparing the data for training models. This step involves cleaning, transforming, and preparing the dataset so that it can be efficiently utilized by ML algorithms. Datasets may contain missing values, outliers, or inconsistencies that need to be addressed. Additionally, one may need to normalize or standardize features to make the data suitable for different algorithms.

2. Overfitting and Underfitting:
Overfitting occurs when a model learns too much from training data and becomes overly specialized, making it perform poorly on unseen data. Underfitting, on the other hand, occurs when a model fails to capture the complexities present in the data and performs poorly even on the training set. Balancing the trade-off between these two extremes can be challenging, and techniques like cross-validation and regularization methods need to be employed to mitigate these issues.

3. Model Selection and Evaluation:
Choosing the right ML model that matches the problem at hand can be daunting. There are various algorithms available, each designed to solve specific tasks and provide different trade-offs. Evaluating the performance of models is also crucial, as it allows us to assess how well the chosen model is generalizing to unseen data. Understanding metrics such as accuracy, precision, recall, or F1-score helps in measuring the model's performance accurately.

4. Feature Selection and Dimensionality:
Determining which features or variables are relevant for a particular ML problem is a skill that requires iteration and experimentation. Sometimes, using irrelevant or unnecessary features can affect the model's performance or introduce redundancy in the data. Feature selection techniques enable us to identify the most informative set of features, whereas dimensionality reduction techniques like Principal Component Analysis (PCA) or Linear Discriminant Analysis (LDA) reduce the number of features while preserving important information.

5. Dealing with Imbalanced Data:
In many real-world scenarios, datasets can have imbalanced class distributions, such as detecting rare diseases or fraud detection. This makes models prone to favor the majority class and perform poorly on minority classes. Techniques like oversampling, undersampling, or their variants, such as SMOTE (Synthetic Minority Oversampling Technique), help in dealing with imbalanced datasets effectively.

6. Computational Resources:
Implementing ML algorithms may require substantial computational resources, especially for complex models and large datasets. Training deep learning models with millions of parameters can be computationally expensive, necessitating access to high-performance hardware resources like Graphics Processing Units (GPUs) or cloud computing platforms. Ensuring system requirements are met is essential to avoid runtime errors or excessive training times.

7. Hyperparameter Tuning:
Almost all ML algorithms have hyperparameters that need to be set before training. These parameters directly affect how the model learns and can dramatically impact its performance. Tuning these hyperparameters to find the optimal configuration is challenging and often requires multiple iterations of training and testing. Techniques like grid search, random search, or advanced optimization algorithms can help in automating the process to some extent.

8. Ethical Considerations and Bias:
Another important challenge is handling ethics and biases within ML applications. ML algorithms learn from the historical data provided to them, and if the training data is biased or contains social, gender, or racial biases, the models can perpetuate and amplify these biases. Recognizing and addressing biases is an ongoing challenge in ML, necessitating diverse datasets, extensive evaluation, and ethical considerations throughout the development process.

9. Interpretability and Explainability:
Machine learning models like deep neural networks are often considered black boxes since they lack transparency, making it challenging to explain why a specific prediction or decision was made. Explainability is crucial in domains like healthcare or self-driving vehicles, where understanding the reasoning behind predictions is essential. Researchers are continuously striving to develop techniques to make ML models more interpretable without sacrificing performance.

10. Deploying ML Models:
The final challenge in machine learning lies in deploying the trained models into real-world applications. Integrating models into existing software systems or developing applications around them requires careful engineering to ensure scalable and efficient solutions. Maintaining models, monitoring their performance, and adapting them to changing requirements is a continuous process that adds to the complexity of deploying ML

applications.

Recognizing these common challenges in machine learning is essential for beginners to have a well-rounded understanding of the field. Overcoming these hurdles involves consistent practice, learning from experience, and adopting best practices while building ML solutions. With dedication and perseverance, anyone can navigate through these challenges and unlock the incredible potential of machine learning.

14.2 Strategies for Overcoming Model Limitations

In the exciting world of machine learning, it is essential to acknowledge that even the most advanced models have certain limitations. Understanding these limitations and knowing how to overcome them is a crucial aspect of building robust and efficient algorithms. Engulfed by this chapter, we will dive into various strategies that can be applied to overcome model limitations. Whether you are a beginner or an expert in the field, these strategies will help you refine your models and maximize their potential.

1. Gather More Data:
One common limitation in machine learning models is insufficient or biased data. By gathering additional data, you increase the chances of capturing essential patterns and overcoming the limitations caused by a small dataset. This approach can enhance the model's performance, reduce bias, and improve generalization.

2. Data Preprocessing:
Preprocessing plays a vital role in machine learning. By cleaning and transforming your data, you improve the quality and accuracy of the models. Techniques like feature scaling, handling missing values, and encoding categorical variables can effectively address limitations associated with messy and unstructured data.

3. Feature Engineering:
Feature engineering involves deriving new features from the existing dataset that can provide more predictive power to the model. It can help overcome limitations such as the curse of dimensionality, where the model struggles due to a high number

of features with little relevance. Techniques such as PCA (Principal Component Analysis), feature selection, and incorporating domain knowledge contribute to feature engineering.

4. Model Selection:
Different algorithms behave differently based on the nature of the problem and the data. If a particular model fails to overcome limitations, it may be worth exploring alternative algorithms. It is important to experiment with a variety of models and assess their performance to select the best one for your specific task.

5. Hyperparameter Tuning:
Models often come with hyperparameters, which are tuning knobs that can significantly impact their performance. By searching for the optimal values of these hyperparameters, we can improve model effectiveness. Techniques such as grid search, random search, and Bayesian optimization can help find the best combination of hyperparameters and tackle limitations related to suboptimal parameter configuration.

6. Regularization:
Overfitting, where the model performs exceptionally well on the training data but fails to generalize to unseen data, is a common limitation. Regularization techniques such as L1 or L2 regularization can add a penalty term to the objective function, avoiding over-reliance on specific features and reducing the model's sensitivity to noise.

7. Ensembling:
Another effective strategy to overcome limitations is creating an ensemble of models. By combining predictions from multiple models, we can reduce bias, increase accuracy, and enhance generalization. Techniques like bagging, boosting, and stacking combine predictions from individual models to leverage their unique strengths and reduce limitations.

8. Cross-validation:
Evaluating the model's performance solely based on its

performance on the training data raises concerns about overfitting. By adopting cross-validation techniques like k-fold or stratified cross-validation, we can obtain a more reliable estimate of the model's capability to generalize. It also helps capture different sources of variation and overcome limitations caused by dataset distribution.

9. Transfer Learning:
Sometimes, the limitation lies in the availability of labeled data for the target task. In such cases, transfer learning can be a powerful strategy. By leveraging knowledge learned from a different but related task, a model can overcome limitations caused by a lack of task-specific training data.

10. Model Evaluation and Monitoring:
Monitoring the model's performance over time is instrumental in identifying its limitations. Regularly evaluating the model's predictions against the actual outcomes allows you to detect limitations that may arise due to concept drift or changes in the data distribution. Implementing automated alerts and systematic evaluations ensures timely intervention and mitigation of these limitations.

These strategies, when applied thoughtfully and systematically, empower you to overcome model limitations, build more robust algorithms, and deploy advanced machine learning solutions. Use them as part of your toolkit as you progress on your journey to mastering machine learning, and keep pushing the boundaries of what is possible.

14.3 Data Quality and Quantity Constraints

In the exciting world of machine learning, understanding the quality and quantity constraints of the data you work with is paramount. As you embark on your journey to become adept in the field, it becomes imperative to have a thorough comprehension of how these constraints can vastly impact the efficacy and results of your machine learning models. This chapter will elucidate the significance of data quality and quantity, equipping you with the knowledge required to navigate these constraints effectively.

Data Quality Constraints:
Data quality is a fundamental pillar that sets the groundwork for any successful machine learning endeavor. Poor data quality can render even the most advanced algorithms futile, leading to erroneous predictions and unreliable models. Here are some crucial factors to consider to ensure high-quality data:

1. Accuracy:
Accurate data is free from errors, inconsistencies, or missing values. It is crucial to closely examine the data sources and employ robust data cleaning techniques, such as removing outliers and addressing missing values, to uphold accuracy.

2. Completeness:
Complete data encompasses having all the necessary attributes for your learning task. Inadequate or missing attributes can undermine the prediction capabilities of your model. You must ascertain that data completeness is maintained through careful data collection and exploration.

3. Consistency:

Consistency relates to the coherence and uniformity of the data across various attributes and instances. Anomalies or contradictions in the data can lead to erratic and less reliable predictions. Scrutinizing the data for inconsistencies and rectifying them is essential for enhancing overall model performance.

4. Relevance:
Data relevance refers to the extent to which the attributes captured in your dataset align with the learning task at hand. It is crucial to curate your dataset meticulously, pruning any irrelevant features that may mislead your model and obscure the overarching patterns.

Data Quantity Constraints:
Apart from ensuring data quality, the quantity of data at your disposal is crucial to improving model performance. Machine learning algorithms often require significant amounts of data to discern meaningful patterns and generalize accurately. Consider the following aspects pertaining to data quantity:

1. Significance of Sample Size:
In machine learning, "bigger is better" tends to hold true for the training dataset. Larger sample sizes generally lead to more reliable and robust models. As you endeavor to expand your dataset, leverage techniques like data augmentation or data synthesis to enrich your pool of instances.

2. Overfitting and Underfitting:
Insufficient data can invite overfitting, where a model becomes too specialized in capturing noise from a limited dataset rather than general characteristics of underlying data distribution. On the other hand, over-abstraction due to a scarcity of data can lead to underfitting, resulting in oversimplified and inaccurate models. Finding the right balance is crucial to optimize model performance.

3. Data Imbalance:
Certain applications of machine learning exhibit class imbalance,

where some classes or labels are overrepresented, and others are underrepresented. This disparity can introduce biases and impede accurate model classification. To combat this, techniques like oversampling, undersampling, and class weighting can address class imbalance.

4. Active Data Collection:
In scenarios where acquiring a substantial labeled dataset is difficult, active data collection techniques can prove valuable. Iteratively selecting and labeling samples based on predictions from existing models allows for focused data collection, facilitating noticeable improvements despite limited resources.

It is important to understand that both data quality and quantity constraints are intertwined, with an overarching goal of empowering your machine learning models to perform effectively and generate reliable insights. Devoting sufficient effort to ensure both data quality and quantity will bring you closer to masterfully undertaking diverse machine learning tasks.

Remember, optimizing these constraints demands continuous learning, evaluation, and adaptation, as no single approach suits all scenarios. Seek new strategies, experiment, and embrace the ever-evolving nature of machine learning. With a firm understanding of data quality and quantity constraints, you possess a solid foundation to embark on your machine learning journey with confidence and poise.

14.4 Continuous Improvement for Sustainable ML

In the world of machine learning, continuous improvement is a vital aspect when it comes to building sustainable models. The iterative nature of machine learning projects demands a constant cycle of learning, improving, and adapting in order to keep up with the ever-changing dynamics of data and ensure the success and performance of your models. Amidst this section, we will delve into the various strategies and approaches that enable continuous improvement for sustainable machine learning projects.

1. Performance Evaluation and Monitoring:
To achieve continuous improvement, it is crucial to regularly evaluate and monitor the performance of a machine learning model. This involves setting up robust performance metrics, such as accuracy, precision, recall, F1 score, and area under the curve (AUC), depending on the problem domain. Through systematic measurement and tracking of these metrics, you can identify areas of improvement and establish a benchmark for comparison with future iterations of your models.

2. Data Quality Assurance:
Data is the lifeblood of any machine learning project, and ensuring its quality is of paramount importance for sustainable ML. Applying data validation techniques like anomaly detection, missing value imputation, and outlier handling helps maintain the integrity and reliability of your datasets. Moreover, data quality assurance involves paying close attention to data bias, ensuring representative data samples, and monitoring drift in data distribution over time, reacting accordingly to maintain the model's performance and fairness.

3. Regular Model Retraining:
As datasets evolve, models may progressively become less effective due to concept drift or changes in the underlying task. To combat this, regular model retraining is necessary. New data can be incorporated to enhance the model's accuracy, and even the model's architecture, hyperparameters, or training techniques can be re-evaluated to improve its performance. In addition, incremental learning and transfer learning techniques can enable retraining by leveraging previously trained models and building upon them to meet new challenges in a resource-efficient manner.

4. Iterative Feature Engineering:
Feature engineering, a crucial aspect of machine learning, involves transforming raw data into meaningful features that facilitate learning by the models. Continuous improvement mandates an ongoing process of analyzing the impact and validity of existing features, incorporating domain knowledge, identifying new sources of valuable information, and experimenting with different feature combinations. By constantly reviewing and enhancing your feature set, you can adapt to ever-changing patterns and improve the overall quality of your models.

5. Feedback Loops and User Feedback:
Gaining valuable feedback from end-users, domain experts, or peers is invaluable for driving continuous improvement in machine learning projects. Feedback loops can capture real-world scenarios, identify performance gaps, suggest potential improvements, and inform feature enhancements. Leveraging methodologies like Active Learning, where models can interactively query real-time feedback, or incorporating user-based information such as ratings or preference observations, enables an iterative process that aligns the models with the actual user requirements.

6. Collaboration and Knowledge Sharing:
Continuous improvement is significantly accelerated when machine learning practitioners actively collaborate and share

their knowledge within communities. Engaging in forums, attending conferences, participating in research groups, and contributing to open-source platforms provides access to diverse perspectives and collective intelligence, fostering innovation, and fueling progress. Engage with others in the field, seek solutions to common challenges, and gain insights from experienced practitioners to bolster your skills and enhance your ML projects.

7. Ethical Considerations:
Continuous improvement cannot be sustained without addressing ethical concerns and implications in machine learning. Responsible AI entails tracking ethical guidelines, staying aware of biases and fairness issues, considering the impact of the model's predictions on various demographic groups, and deploying strategies to mitigate harmful consequences. Continually reassessing, documenting, and auditing the biases and ethical dimensions of your models helps build transparent systems that remain robust and trustworthy throughout their lifespan.

In conclusion, continuous improvement forms the bedrock of sustainable machine learning. By establishing strong performance evaluation and monitoring mechanisms, emphasizing data quality assurance, incorporating regular model retraining, iteratively refining feature engineering, soliciting user feedback, facilitating collaborations, and adhering to ethical norms, you pave the way for a model that evolves harmoniously with your needs and drives impactful and reliable decision-making. Embrace the iterative nature of machine learning and allow continuous improvement to become an inherent part of your ML journey.

Chapter 15: Building a Machine Learning Portfolio

In Chapter 15, we will delve into the crucial aspect of building a machine learning portfolio. As you progress in your journey to become proficient in machine learning, having a portfolio showcasing your work becomes an essential step towards validating your skills and impressing potential employers or clients. Captured within this chapter, we will explore the key considerations, tips, and best practices for constructing an exceptional machine learning portfolio.

1. Importance of a Machine Learning Portfolio:
Having a well-curated portfolio aids in establishing your credibility as a machine learning practitioner. It acts as concrete evidence of your abilities, demonstrating that you understand not only the theoretical concepts but can effectively implement them in real-world scenarios. It helps employers or clients visualize your capabilities and stands as a testament to your commitment to the field.

2. Showcase Your Projects:
When building your portfolio, start by showcasing your machine learning projects. Select a range of projects that highlight your proficiency in various aspects of the discipline. These projects can include supervised or unsupervised learning tasks, classification or regression problems, natural language processing projects, computer vision tasks, or even advanced applications like deep learning or reinforcement learning.

3. Document Project Details:
For each project in your portfolio, provide a comprehensive description to convey the objectives, methodologies employed, and outcomes achieved. Include details on the dataset(s) used,

any preprocessing techniques applied, the machine learning algorithms implemented, and the evaluation metrics utilized. Supplement this with charts, graphs, or visuals to add visual appeal and enhance understanding.

4. Collaborative Projects:
Engaging in collaborative projects demonstrates your ability to work effectively as part of a team, an immensely valuable skill in the industry. Include projects where you worked in partnership with others, highlighting the collaborative aspects and the contributions you made to the team's success.

5. Contributions to the Community:
Actively participating in the machine learning community showcases your dedication to continuous learning and growth. Include any open-source projects, contributions to popular machine learning libraries, or involvement in online discussion forums such as Kaggle. Highlight any awards or recognition received in these areas, as they add credibility to your profile.

6. Visualization and Code samples:
Effectively communicating your work is essential. Showcase your ability to present complex machine learning concepts in an easily understandable manner by including attractive and informative visualizations. Alongside that, share links to your code repositories or provide snippets of your code, offering a glance into your programming prowess.

7. Experimentation and Innovation:
Don't shy away from experimenting with cutting-edge techniques or novel ideas. Including such projects in your portfolio demonstrates your willingness to push boundaries and explore uncharted territories. Moreover, it gives potential employers a glimpse of your creativity, problem-solving skills, and ability to think outside the box.

8. Documentation and Process:
Highlighting your proficiency in documenting your work and adhering to a structured process enhances your professional

reliability. Discuss your approach to data exploration, feature engineering, model selection, hyperparameter tuning, and validation techniques. Outlining a clear methodology with rigorous evaluations provides further evidence of your competence.

9. Continuous Learning:
Machine learning is a rapidly evolving field, and staying on top of the latest advancements is vital. In your portfolio, emphasize your commitment to ongoing learning through professional development courses, workshops, or certifications. This illustrates your proactive attitude and dedication to staying updated with emerging trends.

10. Refine and Polish:
Creating an excellent portfolio takes time and effort. Continuously refine and polish your completed projects, ensuring that all details are accurate, crisp, and fully encompassing. Usability and understandability should be key considerations as you organize projects within your portfolio, ensuring potential reviewers can easily navigate and absorb information.

Building a machine learning portfolio requires creativity, high attention to detail, and the ability to convey complex concepts in a simplified manner. It serves as an opportunity to demonstrate your skills, stand out from the competition, and leave a lasting impression on potential employers or clients. By constructing a well-rounded, diverse, and comprehensive portfolio, you significantly enhance your chances of success in the exciting field of machine learning.

15.1 Importance of a Machine Learning Portfolio

In the ever-expanding field of machine learning, building a strong portfolio is of utmost significance for beginners. As aspiring machine learning practitioners, it is crucial to understand the importance of showcasing your skills and projects through a well-crafted portfolio. Within this section, we will delve into the reasons why a machine learning portfolio is valuable, and how it can play a significant role in your career or educational journey.

1. Demonstrate Practical Skills: A machine learning portfolio provides tangible evidence of your abilities as a practitioner. It allows you to exhibit your technical skills, problem-solving capabilities, and proficiency in implementing machine learning algorithms. By showcasing actual projects, you provide potential employers or educational institutions with concrete examples of your work, highlighting your ability to apply theoretical knowledge to real-world challenges.

2. Showcase Creativity and Innovation: Your portfolio serves as a platform to display your creativity and innovation. Machine learning algorithms offer a wide range of applications, from natural language processing to computer vision and beyond. Utilizing your portfolio, you can exhibit your unique approaches to solving problems, demonstrating your ability to think outside the box and generate novel solutions. This showcases your potential for contributing original ideas to the field.

3. Reflect Continuous Learning: Machine learning portfolios provide insight into your learning journey. As a beginner, your portfolio may document prototypes, projects, or experiments that highlight your progress. It serves as a visual representation

of the learning curve you have undergone – from your initial analyses to more sophisticated models. This demonstrates your commitment to continuous learning, adaptability, and growth within the field.

4. Build Credibility and Trust: An influential machine learning portfolio establishes credibility in your abilities and enhances trustworthiness among potential employers, collaborators, or academic institutions. When faced with various candidates, a well-structured portfolio showcasing your accomplishments can differentiate you from others, providing solid evidence of your skills and boosting your professional or academic reputation.

5. Network Expansion: Having a compelling portfolio enables you to network effectively within the machine learning community. By sharing your work on platforms such as GitHub, Kaggle, or personal websites, you create opportunities for interacting with experienced practitioners and researchers. As your reputation grows, you become more likely to receive collaboration offers, research proposals, mentorship invitations, and even job opportunities from individuals or organizations impressed by your work.

6. Targeting Specific Goals: A machine learning portfolio also allows you to align your projects with personal, professional, or educational goals. By carefully selecting projects that emphasize particular aspects or domains of machine learning, you can tailor your portfolio to meet specific objectives. Whether you aim to pursue advanced research, gain industry recognition, or secure admission into prestigious schools, a well-curated portfolio will help you showcase the relevant skills and expertise required for those targets.

7. Learn and Improve: Constructing your machine learning portfolio provides a powerful self-learning opportunity. As you accumulate and present your projects, you inevitably review and critique your work, leading to iterative improvements of your code, analysis techniques, presentation skills, and documentation. This iterative process helps you reflect on your

work, identify areas for growth, and refine your thought processes, thereby enhancing your overall portfolio and competence as a machine learning practitioner.

Remember, a machine learning portfolio is not fixed in stone. It continues to evolve as you complete new projects, gain additional knowledge, and broaden your abilities. Consistently updating and improving your portfolio is vital to stay relevant and attractive to potential employers or educational institutions.

In conclusion, developing a machine learning portfolio is crucial for showcasing your skills, creativity, and growth within the field. A well-crafted portfolio not only sets you apart from others but also serves as a catalyst for networking opportunities, collaboration, and professional advancement. Embrace the process of building and refining your portfolio as it both solidifies your understanding of machine learning concepts and exemplifies your contributions to the field.

15.2 Showcasing Projects and Practical Applications

Machine learning is a powerful field that has revolutionized various industries and sectors, making it an exciting time for beginners to dive into this domain. As you progress in your understanding of machine learning fundamentals, it's important to explore projects and practical applications to witness the potential of this technology firsthand. Housed within this chapter, we will walk through some exhilarating projects and real-life applications that effectively demonstrate the power and versatility of machine learning algorithms.

1. Image Classification:
Develop an image classifier using convolutional neural networks (CNN) to categorize images into different classes. For instance, you can build a model to classify vehicles, animals, or even distinguish between various object categories with high accuracy. Utilize popular datasets like ImageNet or CIFAR-10, and experiment with different neural network architectures to enhance your model's performance.

2. Sentiment Analysis:
Dive into natural language processing and sentiment analysis using recurrent neural networks (RNN) or transformer models. Develop a sentiment classifier that can predict emotions or opinions expressed in text. Implement this model on social media data, movie reviews, or customer feedback to gauge sentiment and comprehend the overall perception towards specific topics or products.

3. Fraud Detection:
Explore the fascinating world of anomaly detection and fraud mitigation techniques using machine learning. Build a model on

a dataset containing labeled fraudulent and regular transactions, and utilize algorithms such as Isolation Forest, decision trees, or neural networks to identify instances of fraudulent activity. Witness how machine learning can significantly enhance fraud prevention in banking, e-commerce, or any domain dealing with transactions.

4. Recommendation Systems:
Dig into the nuances of collaborative filtering and content-based recommendation systems. Create a personalized movie recommender system that analyzes user preferences and suggests relevant films. Use popular techniques such as matrix factorization or deep learning approaches to construct accurate and efficient recommendation systems. This project showcases how machine learning algorithms can decipher complex user preferences and provide tailored recommendations.

5. Autonomous Driving:
Venture into the realm of autonomous vehicles and explore how machine learning plays a critical role in this domain. Simulate an autonomous driving environment using frameworks like CARLA or AirSim and develop deep learning models to accurately detect and track objects such as pedestrians, vehicles, and traffic signs. Showcase how machine learning can enable safe and efficient autonomous transportation systems.

6. Medical Diagnostics:
Discover the breakthrough potential of machine learning algorithms in the healthcare sector. Build a diagnostic system that analyzes medical images, such as X-rays or MRI scans, to detect diseases and abnormalities. Construct a deep learning architecture like U-Net or utilize pre-trained models and fine-tuning techniques to accurately identify conditions like pneumonia, tumors, or anomalies in radiological images.

7. Chatbots:
Delve into natural language processing and build a conversational chatbot using techniques like sequence-to-sequence models or transformers. Create a chatbot that

understands and responds to user queries, providing relevant and helpful information. Implement this chatbot on websites or messaging platforms to offer automated customer support and discover how machine learning enhances human-computer interactions.

8. Stock Price Prediction:
Use historical stock market data and machine learning techniques to predict future stock prices. Employ algorithms like recurrent neural networks (RNN) or long short-term memory (LSTM) models to analyze patterns, market indicators, and news sentiment so as to forecast stock prices. Explore the challenges and opportunities in this domain, all while showcasing the potential role of machine learning in financial markets.

These projects and applications are demonstrations of the immense potential behind machine learning algorithms. By embarking on these hands-on experiences, you will gain invaluable insights into the intricacies of various techniques and appreciate the wide-reaching impact of machine learning across diverse industries. Encourage creativity and exploration as you build these projects, and never hesitate to dive deeper into the concepts and methodologies to enhance your understanding. Get ready to unleash the power of machine learning and pave the way for a future of intelligent technology.

15.3 Documenting Model Development Process

15.3 Documenting Model Development Process
In the field of machine learning, documentation plays a crucial role in capturing the development process of building models. Documenting the steps and decisions made during the models' creation is advantageous for several reasons. Firstly, it helps in better collaboration among team members by providing a comprehensive understanding of the model development process. Secondly, it improves reproducibility, enabling others to recreate the model and build upon it. Lastly, it serves as a valuable resource for future reference, analysis, and potential model enhancements. Within the context of this section, we will explore the importance of documenting the model development process and delve into key components to consider.

1. Model Overview:
Begin by providing a high-level overview of the model, highlighting its purpose, desired outcomes, and intended use. This ensures that readers understand the context and objectives of the model before diving into the details.

2. Data Collection:
Discuss the methods employed to collect relevant data for training and testing the machine learning model. This includes highlighting the data sources, methodologies used, and any preprocessing steps involved, such as data cleaning, feature engineering, or augmentation techniques.

3. Data Analysis:
Detail the exploratory data analysis (EDA) techniques utilized to gain insights into the collected dataset. Explain the statistical methods employed, visualization approaches used, and any

patterns or trends discovered during the analysis phase. Showing visual representations of key findings alongside descriptive explanations can significantly enhance the clarity of the documentation.

4. Model Selection:
Explain the rationale behind the chosen machine learning algorithm(s) for model development. Elaborate on why specific models were considered, highlighting their strengths and weaknesses in relation to the problem at hand. Providing theoretical justifications or empirical comparisons between different algorithms can offer valuable insights.

5. Model Design:
Illustrate in-depth how the chosen model was designed, including its architecture, hyperparameters, and any optimization techniques employed. Provide detailed explanations of the model's structure, highlighting the role and function of each component. Pseudocode or code snippets can aid in implementation clarity.

6. Model Training:
Describe the training process, emphasizing the methodology, techniques, and strategies implemented. Discuss the training dataset, validation approaches used for model evaluation, and any cross-validation or early stopping procedures. Present the training hyperparameters and their influence on model performance, backed by empirical evidence or experiment results.

7. Model Evaluation:
Outline the metrics and evaluation techniques used to assess the model's performance. Provide a comprehensive analysis of the model's accuracy, precision, recall, F1-score, or any other relevant metrics specific to the problem domain. Discuss the potential biases or limitations of the evaluation process, including any external factors that may influence the assessments.

8. Model Deployment:
Discuss the considerations, challenges, and techniques involved in deploying and operationalizing the model. Explain any modifications or alterations necessary when transitioning from development to production environments. Include infrastructure requirements, considerations for real-time predictions, and any integration details with existing systems.

9. Documentation Standards:
Introduce any standardized formats, templates, or guidelines for documenting the model development process within your organization or the broader machine learning community. These standards ensure consistency across projects and facilitate robust collaboration among researchers and developers.

10. Ethical Considerations:
Address ethical concerns associated with the development, deployment, or usage of the model. Discuss potential biases, fairness issues, or unintended consequences that may emerge. Emphasize the importance of ethical evaluation and continual monitoring of the model's behavior after deployment.

11. Challenges and Lessons Learned:
Reflect on challenges encountered during the model development process and discuss how they were overcome. Share valuable lessons learned from your experience, both in terms of technical aspects and project management. Providing real-world anecdotes or case studies can make the documentation more relatable and engaging.

Conclusion:
Summarize the key takeaways from the documented model development process. Reinforce the significance of comprehensive documentation for knowledge sharing, collaboration, reproducibility, and future advancements. Encourage readers to adopt similar practices while fostering an environment of continuous learning and improvement within the machine learning community.

By thoroughly documenting the model development process, individuals can glean valuable insights for refining existing models and developing new ones. Additionally, these documented insights serve as an educational resource, enabling beginners to understand the intricacies of machine learning and fostering the growth of the field as a whole.

15.4 Enhancing Employability with a Strong ML Portfolio

Enhancing Employability with a Strong ML Portfolio

In today's competitive job market, having a strong machine learning (ML) portfolio is crucial to stand out from the crowd and increase your employability in this rapidly evolving field. A comprehensive ML portfolio not only showcases your technical capabilities but also demonstrates your practical experience in solving real-world problems using ML techniques. Amidst the details of this chapter, we will explore how to effectively build and showcase your ML portfolio to maximize your professional prospects.

1. Understand the Significance of a ML Portfolio:
Before diving into the process of creating a machine learning portfolio, it's important to understand why it holds such significance. Employers often hesitate to prioritize resumes that lack concrete evidence of hands-on ML experience. A well-constructed portfolio provides tangible proof of your ability to implement ML algorithms, experiment with data, extract meaningful insights, and communicate them effectively. A solid portfolio acts as a testament to your skills and helps potential employers assess your capabilities with more confidence.

2. Select Relevant ML Projects:
One crucial aspect of building an ML portfolio is choosing the right projects that align with your interests and potential job opportunities. Selecting diverse and relevant projects enables you to showcase your proficiency in various ML techniques and their applications in different domains. Start by brainstorming potential projects that inspire you and have real-world implications. Consider working on projects that tackle problems

you care about, such as recommender systems, fraud detection, image recognition, or natural language processing. Aim to strike a balance between projects that highlight a range of ML algorithms, data preprocessing techniques, and evaluation metrics.

3. Data Collection and Preprocessing:
Once you have identified your project ideas, gather suitable datasets that can serve as the foundation for your explorations. Evaluate whether the selected datasets are representative of the problem domain and possess attributes that challenge you to employ different ML methods. Additionally, ensure the datasets are clean, consistent, and truly reflective of real-world scenarios by thoroughly pre-processing them through techniques like data cleaning, feature engineering, normalization, and outlier handling. A solid foundation in data collection and preprocessing showcases your ability to work with messy datasets and extract valuable insights.

4. Model Development and Evaluation:
Now that you have prepared your datasets, it's time to dive into algorithm implementation. Begin by selecting appropriate ML algorithms based on the nature of the problem and the characteristics of the data. Experiment with different algorithms, hyperparameters, and feature selection techniques to optimize your models' performance. Leverage common ML libraries such as scikit-learn, TensorFlow, or PyTorch to implement your solutions efficiently. Ensure you rigorously evaluate the trained models using established metrics such as accuracy, precision, recall, or F1-score. Clearly document your experimental process, keeping track of the models you've built, hyperparameters used, and their corresponding evaluation results.

5. Visualize Results and Insights:
When presenting your ML projects, visualization plays a crucial role in facilitating the understanding and interpretation of complex results. Explore various ways to visualize your models' performance, the distribution of data, or feature importance. Effective and aesthetic visualizations enhance your portfolio's

readability and demonstrate your ability to effectively communicate your findings to diverse audiences. Utilize visualization libraries such as Matplotlib, Seaborn, or Plotly to create captivating visual representations that highlight the essence of your ML projects.

6. Document Your Process:
Carefully document your entire ML journey, beginning from the formulation of the problem statement to the final implementation. Maintain well-organized project folders that consist of the datasets used, the code files, including preprocessing steps, model training, and evaluation scripts. It's beneficial to include a concise summary and explanation of each project, describing the motivation behind the project, the problem statement, and the main findings. Keep track of the challenges you encountered, the strategies you adopted to overcome them, and the iterative steps that molded the final outcome. Highlight any novel approaches or methodologies you incorporated to demonstrate your creativity and ability to think outside the box.

7. Communicate Effectively:
Possessing technical skills alone is not sufficient. Effective communication skills can considerably enhance your employability in the field of ML. Write detailed and articulate explanations accompanying your project documentation to communicate your thought process, rationale behind decision-making, and the impacts of your results. Practice summarizing your projects in a clear, concise, and non-technical manner during interviews or networking events. Developing the ability to communicate complex ML concepts to both technical and non-technical stakeholders demonstrates your aptitude to collaborate within multidisciplinary teams.

8. Explore Collaborative Opportunities:
To further strengthen your ML portfolio and demonstrate your ability to work within teams, consider engaging in collaborative opportunities. Participate in open-source projects, join online ML competitions, or team up with other aspiring ML enthusiasts

on platforms like Kaggle to jointly solve complex problems. Collaboration not only showcases your teamwork and problem-solving skills but also exposes you to diverse perspectives and methodologies in ML.

9. Stay Updated and Curious:
The field of machine learning is continuously evolving with new algorithms, frameworks, and methodologies emerging regularly. To stay ahead, it's essential to cultivate a habit of continuous learning and curiosity. Stay updated with recent research papers, attend conferences, and participate in webinars or workshops to keep pace with the latest developments in ML. Continually expanding your knowledge and skills demonstrates your dedication to staying on top of industry trends and your endless pursuit of excellence.

By following these guidelines and investing time into crafting a comprehensive ML portfolio, you enable potential employers to recognize your value, making you more marketable in the competitive ML job market. Remember, building a strong ML portfolio goes beyond showcasing technical expertise. It also showcases your ability to think critically, solve problems, and effectively communicate your findings—an essential combination for success in this exciting and ever-evolving field.

Printed in Great Britain
by Amazon